Hedley

22 Is My Lu(

Copyright © 2020 Hedley Kirkman

All rights reserved.

ISBN: 9798644704972

Hope you enjoy the
read Annie
Clive 07789 02548

DEDICATION

Dedicated to my loving family, the rehab where my recovery began and to my friends now in and outside the fellowship.

CONTENTS

Acknowledgments

22 Is my Lucky Number

My Early Working Life and Travels

Further Studies, Work and Travels

Back Home, Work and Business

Difficult Times and a Miracle

Marriage, Work and Rock Bottom

Recovery and a New Life

Faith, Recovery and Some Mistakes

About the Author

ACKNOWLEDGMENTS

Many thanks to; -

Wonderdog Publishing for designing, producing and publishing this work.

Wonderdog Publishing
07812 126 144

Hedley Kirkman

Isiah Chapter 22, Verse 22

"I place on his shoulder the key to the house of David; what he opens no one can shut and what he shuts no one can open."

22 IS MY LUCKY NUMBER

When I think of my life as a child, they are mostly happy memories with loving parents and a paradise in the way of the surroundings. I say it was a paradise as it was a beautiful vegetable farm of some two hundred acres and a Grade 2 listed farmhouse. There was also a one acre vegetable and fruit garden plus an acre of flower gardens with lawns and a moat beyond which was a tennis court, a large rockery and more fruit trees. It was in Hornchurch, Essex near the suburbs of London and went by the intriguing name of Lillyputts and was on Wingletye Lane. I could roam to my heart's content when not at school. My two favourite pastimes were to play in ponds catching newts and water boatmen etc and putting them in an aquarium behind one of the stables so they were in the shade. Another was at the age of about eight, I started gardening on my own, growing vegetables and propagating plants such as Lavender which seemed easier in those days! Today the farm would be considered organic, my dad used no chemicals, we had four pairs of working horses and a colt to cart the vegetables from the field. I also used to help my mum in the flower garden. With the abundance of all these vegetables and fruit, we ate healthily. My favourite meal (among many!) was gammon and potatoes, green peas and young carrots and of course, with parsley sauce! On other occasions we would have lamb with redcurrant jelly which my mum used to make. I was spoilt in so many ways… I remember two particular things about the gardens as they had too many special features to mention. One is the asparagus beds which were kept immaculately and produced mouthwatering spears. The beds were about half a metre high, two metres wide and two beds of about eight metres in length. The other is a summerhouse which was fairly unique – well, I have never seen another like it! It could be rotated according to the direction of the sun. On the warmer days, my mum would often put me in there for an afternoon nap when I was a young child. Next to it was a Mulberry tree, the healthiest I have ever seen. It had been pollarded many years ago and stood perhaps twenty metres tall and twenty metres across. From this healthy outdoor lifestyle, the seed was sown for me to grow plants in later life as a profession.

Unfortunately, my mum did not have such an easy upbringing. Her father was a domineering and arrogant bully who just lived for money. This caused both her and her mum to be of a nervous disposition, both having neuralgia on their cheeks. When my sister, two years older than me, and myself were born, she could not, for health reasons, be a full time mum. So, we had a nanny named Florrie who was like our surrogate mum. Not being able to pronounce things very well in those days, I used to call her 'Frolfrigs' and I was always under her feet! Both my sister and I were sent to boarding school. My sister went at eleven and me at aged nine. My sister found this difficult to accept but I understood that they wanted the best for us.

I remember hearing my sister say, "You're sending me away because you don't love me!" I was a particularly shy boy so I suffered when I first went to boarding school. I was so shy when I was first there that I would not ask where the toilets were so, after two or three days, I wet the bed. However, it was a good school and surprisingly, there was no bullying. As I find in life, it is full of opposites. Amazingly, despite my loving parents and lovely surroundings, I would mistakenly turn around and tell them during the summer holidays, that I was bored! I still have that problem today. Despite being shy, I was quite a naughty boy and was very lucky not to be expelled from school. I would get up to all sorts of pranks and I was lucky to not be found out. I will give you a couple of examples of my pranks. My parents gave me a chemistry set when I was still in junior school. This was lovely for me and I would make stink bombs and play with the chemicals as they would precipitate out to make kaleidoscope of colours. This interest led me to do well in my Chemistry O level. My other stunts were a bit more worrying, especially my fascination with fire. These things I would do on my own. So, while at junior school, I set light to rolls of newspaper under the cellar so the smoke came up through the floorboards. A roll call was made and questions were asked. I kept my powder dry and nobody snitched on me although I was not a large boy. On another occasion I set fire to one of the barns on the farm by accident and my dad did not even beat me. Later, I nearly set fire to the paraffin tank as I lit the ground where the paraffin was leaking. I got myself into a right panic before I managed to put it out. Another stunt at school was when I was in senior school. I got up one night and went to the print room. I was surprised to find it unlocked. I found the mock exam papers, made about four copies of each subject and handed them out to my friends. We all got results of over 90% which raised a few eyebrows! Once again, I got away with it...

I was perhaps around fifteen when my mum told me that my dad had terminal cancer. When I think of my family in those early years, quite a long time ago now, I think of my dad as a very humble and loving man. He was a true gentleman in the full sense of the word, so different to my grandfather. My mum did her best under difficult circumstances as I have already mentioned. My dad, although Conservative, had a very broad outlook upon life. For example, he loved the songs of Paul Robeson who, as we know, was a Communist and was restricted in where he could travel. He was very hard working and when we went on holiday for two weeks, he would always come back to the farm two or three times to check on the crops etc. So, news of our dad's impending death must have been devastating, especially for my mum, but she stood strong. She did the most loving things for my father, that were within her power. Instead of him spending is last days in hospital, he was nursed 24/7. He had a strong heart and lived longer than expected. As was traditional in those days, he was not told that he had cancer but was told that he had suffered a stroke and was without the use of one arm due to the trauma on his brain. The experience had a profound effect on me and no longer did I play the prankster at school, instead I started to study hard. I knew that academically I was not that clever. I decided to just do my O levels, as they were called in those days, then just leave school. Also, I did not want to be a financial burden on my mum although I found out later that it was my grandfather who paid the school fees. I gained seven O levels, two in Maths and four A grades in my favourite subjects, Chemistry, History, Geography and Religious Knowledge. This somewhat surprised the headmaster I believe!

I mention my sister only briefly. She was two years older than me and did not have much of an impact on my life, partly because we were sent away. The only thing I remember in particular was that I tried to protect her from dodgy boyfriends as they often used to try and be friends with her through me. She decided, after leaving school, to become a nurse but prior to going for training she went on a secretarial course in case she found that nursing wasn't for her. In the event that turned out to be the case as she did find that nursing wasn't for her as she couldn't stand the sight of blood in the operating theatre! But she managed to carve out a good career as a medical secretary, which I will come back to later.

As my dad had old fashioned ideas when it came to the depression in the 1930's, he got himself into some debt and instead of borrowing money, he chose to sell the farm so it was rented from then on. When it came to his death, everything had to go as I was not old enough if I had decided to take over from him. It was not something that I was seriously interested in anyway as I noted that a lot of the produce was being returned unsold, which must have been heartbreaking for my dad after having put in all the work. In the meantime my mum found a nice, smaller farmhouse called Thorpe Cross Farmhouse near Frinton on Sea in Essex which is near Thorpe-Le- Soken. I was able to drive by then and helped her to move some of the smaller items with a van we had borrowed from family friends. When she moved, our grandfather and grandmother came to live with her which must have helped financially. They had lived with us for a while at Lillyputts but dad couldn't abide his uncouth behavior so they were asked to leave and move to a house near Bexhill-On-Sea. She looked after them until they passed away. By this time, I was courting or away at college although I used to visit quite a lot at weekends.

Whilst at school I had three or four good friends. I have happy memories of these friends and have a folder in my flat containing a cartoon that a friend drew of the three of us. I had straw growing out of my hair being the farmers boy! I had a strange, briefly homosexual relationship with one of these boys. I was perhaps only ten years old and we would go to bed together until disturbed when the house master came on his rounds. It was not an intensive relationship and, for me, was natural at the time. I used to go home at weekends every two weeks or so and when that didn't happen, a friend's parents used to take us out in their Morgan car. In the summer we used to enjoy ice cream together. One weekend when my parents visited, we visited an antique shop up the road in Chigwell where we bought a small bowl which we still have in the family today.

MY EARLY WORKING LIFE AND TRAVELS

As I mentioned earlier, my interest was plants in general but later became flowers and shrubs in particular. So it was that this seed sales representative, who used to sell vegetable seeds to my dad, found me a job as an apprentice. This was with a local large seed company called Hurst Gunson Cooper Taber which at that time was owned by a Hungarian Jewish family. This seed representative and his wife became family friends. I started, as it was Autumn, in the bulb department. My mum decided, as a nice gesture, which influenced my thinking later in life, to give some daffodil bulbs to the school where I boarded. After working in the bulb department for a while I moved to the vegetables and flower seed department. To be honest, at this young age, I was not much use as these orders had to be accurate as, especially some of the flower seeds, were expensive. As a result, I often ended up sweeping the floor or making the tea. After that I went to the vegetable trial which was a happier time as I was outside and at one with nature tending the various crops. Everything was grown to a high standard as not only had the vegetables to be on trial but farmers would come to view the trials with the idea of purchasing seeds. They were often shown around by their local representative. I was also understudy to the vegetable breeder who was clever, introducing new peas, sprouts, tomatoes and cabbage etc. Anything with Kelvedon in its name (such as Kelvedon Wonder Pea) would come from the trial ground. They also had a flower breeder who also bred sweet corn. But I was too young and perhaps, too immature so I got itchy feet... I decided to go to college and do a Horticultural diploma course Essex is very financially supportive of the college,

Writtle, where we went. So, I received a grant that not only paid my tuition fees but also gave me an allowance for my accommodation etc. Plus, in those days it was easy to get holiday jobs and this was useful work experience as I was still wet behind the ears! I was not offered accommodation on the campus as I was a local Essex boy, instead, we were given a list of local landladies. The first one I think I checked proved to be more than ideal. The lady had become widowed and treated me like her own son. I had breakfast with her and my evening meal. I was very happy there and it was only a short walk to the college. I found the studies stimulating as well as the practical work. I realised, with hindsight, that my experience of having worked made it easier for me to relate to what was taught in the lectures. Most of the students had come straight from doing A levels and so had no work experience. Of course, the sons and daughters of farmers or smallholders were also at an advantage. In the second year, a fellow student who I had become friends with, came to live with the same landlady. Around this time, I developed a friendship with two other students and we had quite an active social life although I was still really shy at that age. This involve, on occasions, going to visit my sister and her nursing friends at Lancaster Gate near Hyde Park in London. We were brave and drove there! At this time my sister was working at Bart's hospital as a medical secretary to a team of surgeons. All three of us fell in love with girls there and one friend took a liking to my sister but she was not interested. I fell in love with a natural, red headed freckled girl from Ireland who came from a well off family. I took her, as one of the group, to the first college summer ball which was a lovely occasion. Playing that night was Jimmy Cliff who amazingly still sings today. It was the tradition to pick strawberries in the nearby fields. On parting with her I cried, as I guessed that I would not see her again and so it proved to be but a happy memory.

When staying with my mum I found the Young Farmers Club and went to meetings and social events. Again, I fell in love but with a farmer's daughter this time. On this occasion there was competition which I had to eventually let go of as I was not ready for settling down. She eventually married a farmer and later I worked for him and his dad during the summer holidays, so there was no animosity. However, I did have the opportunity to take her to the second summer ball at our college so that is another happy memory.

One college friend, Pete, and myself made plans to emigrate to Canada and it was then, when I went to the High Commission for a medical, that I was told that I needed to wear glasses. We actually had no plan to emigrate but it was just that we could get free flights if we told them that we wanted to emigrate! Pete's father was a fruit farmer and they had quite a few contacts in Canada. One couple were my uncle Dan and an auntie. I don't know to this day whether they were related or it was just a term of endearment, but I think the latter. So, initially we went to stay and I used it as a base when I was working or preparing for my travels. They gave us both a lot of useful advice. I guess they must have advised us to go about 50 kilometers North to a little area called Little Holland to seek work. The name is self-explanatory as it was a peaty area where various crops were grown by families from Holland that had settled there. The crops included carrot, onions and tobacco. I think, after hitch hiking to the area, we were accepted by the farm we first approached. It was run by Frank Weening and his family. We started off working in the carrot crop. They treated us like family and we had our meals with them. After a couple of weeks, Pete went off apple picking further North through a contact he had. I stayed with the Weening family with the idea of picking tobacco but I only did a day of that! Frank then asked me to be a kiln hand which I only accepted because it paid good money. It was quite an unpleasant job as I shall go on to relate. I had to hang the lathes of leaves as they went up a conveyor belt, trying to take care not to miss or fall through the rafters resulting in a nasty fall. It was a hot and sticky job up there and you got covered in a slimy green/brown gunge. After a day's work you looked like a Leprechaun! After all of this, my clothes were only good enough to throw into the bin! After I finished that job I went back to Toronto and my uncle Dan found me a job in Brampton, near Toronto, with a seed firm. He was a lawyer for the firm. It was one late Sunday afternoon when he took me to the warehouse office and I camped out at night so I was first to work in the morning. It was hard graft and I didn't enjoy it very much. Most of the workers were Italian so I didn't really have anyone to converse with. After work I was recommended some lodgings. It was a couple and I can't remember whether they had any children or not. What I do remember is that they rowed a lot and he had a habit of drinking while driving which I adopted later in life. I will come back to this later. From there I went further North and met up with Pete again. We went contract pruning with that same contact of his called Ken Coates. He was quite a shrewd operator and taught us all the tricks of the trade. We were paid so much per tree and Pete was a bit faster than me. We were working in temperatures around -20C. being young and stupid, I wore no earmuffs so developed chilblains on my ears. This troubled me for sure, even when I was working outside in Milton Keynes quite a few years later but it is no problem today. There was a good thickness of snow on the ground so there was no problem climbing up into the trees. While doing the pruning we found lodgings with a local family. They had a daughter who Pete fell in love with. Amazingly, Ken called her 'Pasty Face' as her skin was so white, like a ghost!

Talking of falling in love, that happened to me when working with the Weenings. One Saturday, shortly after we had arrived, a picnic was organised by the local Christian community. The idea was that the girls would prepare a picnic hamper and us boys would enter a raffle to see which girls we would picnic with. Well, I was in luck that day as I was to be with a lovely girl called Rita Kribbe. She was a natural blonde with an open face and a body to match! She also had a very pleasant personality.

Some years later, when I spoke to Pete about it, he admitted to being quite jealous of me! Next, a marathon was organised back to Toronto. I thought I would see Rita and run beside her. Well, I did see her but she ran so fast that I never saw her again!

After several months of pruning, both Pete and I had saved enough money to set off on our travels again which, for some reason, we did separately. Pete went to work in Vancouver and then went on to travel in Alaska where he met his now, wife. I purchased a $99 Greyhound bus pass which lasted for three months and so I made my plans for where I would like to visit. Places of historic or educational interest and of course, places of beauty and horticultural interest. The only places I decided not to visit were Florida and Alaska as I already had enough on my plate. It was perhaps in late April that I set off and the first place to visit was Vermont to Cardwell University which was a lovely, grey stone campus which sat nicely against the blue sky and the green landscape. It must have been spectacular in Autumn with the trees wearing their Autumn colours. From there I went to Boston and visited some of the historic sites. The next stop was Washington DC where Pete had put me in touch with some of his friends who I was able to with. This was a nice rest as it was my habit to travel overnight sometimes to save hotel costs. I would do this for one or two nights and then have a rest and stay in a hotel. It was all carefully planned. I struck Washington at an ideal time. The skies were blue and the pink cherry blossom was in full bloom which contrasted nicely with the white monuments and the blue Potomac river. With Bink and his wife we made a trip to Williamsburg, an old colonial town, where I took a few photos. After saying my goodbyes to Bink and his wife, I set off to North Carolina where the Azaleas and Cornus trees were in full bloom. Auntie Pat had said that I should send them postcards as I went about my travels and she would give them to me upon my return so that I would have memories of my travels. This I did and I still have those postcards today. Being a fan of country music, I set off from North Carolina to

Nashville, Tennessee. Although I didn't go to the Old Oprey, I soaked up the atmosphere and enjoyed the short stay very much. After that it was off to New Orleans via Baton Rouge. I found it hot and sticky there and didn't like the dust very much so I didn't stay too long. With hindsight, maybe I didn't sample enough of the food there to make a judgement. It was then on to Pueblo where I visited friends and admired the traditional Pueblo houses. Next, it was on to the Grand Canyon, one of the many highlights of my trip. I arrived during the day and found some simple accommodation close to the Canyon itself. After a good night's sleep, I got up in the morning to find it frosty and dry. Down into the canyon I went all by myself, meeting nobody else there at that early hour. I got to the Indian garden which I guess was about halfway down. That had lovely views, both down to the Colorado and back to the stunning rock formations as they reflected the rising sun. I could see the Colorado river which I believe is substantially dried up now due to dams and irrigation upstream in California. After this it was off to El Paso and just briefly, across the border into Mexico to sample a taste of the culture. I found the atmosphere very relaxing and friendly. One might say that they're after the tourist's money but I disagree and think it's more than that. I bought a small, leather embossed briefcase which was nice but hardly ever used. Upon leaving El Paso, I went further West to Los Angeles. I didn't stay long because the lady I was going to see was busy at the time. I guess that she was a contact that I had been given along the way. Off I went then to Santa Barbara where I decided to sleep on the beach. Not the best idea as it was rather damp and cold and I did not get a good night's sleep. Next was Yosemite of which I have lasting and pleasant memories. I shared accommodation with fellow travellers, not my way as I did my travelling on my own. The rock formations and general landscape were quite spectacular with glacial formations with evergreen and deciduous forests below. Added to this was a two stage waterfall leading to a stream which I have photograph of. Down in the forest you could imagine that you were in the Garden Of Eden but without the apples! Off I went then to San Francisco with its pleasant and special appeal and I stayed for two or three days. The first thing I did was to explore the city using the unique tram system. I had to be quite robust as San Francisco is quite an undulating city. I enjoyed the parks and museums. The other 'must do' is the Golden Gate Bridge where, on a fine day, you can view the twin city of Oakland. I guess I must have hitched there and back. Unfortunately, it was time to think about getting back to L.A. where there was a lady waiting to show me around. She was very nice to me and we walked along Sunset Boulevard and then onto the Hollywood Studios. I watched some of the action there. She took me to Hollywood to see where the stars and directors live, I saw Bing Crosby out jogging! Of course, before leaving L.A. I had to visit the original Disneyland and what an absolute thrill that was! It's such a long time ago now, it's difficult to remember everything, although I do know that I visited Frontierland and Waterland. Then it was back North to briefly visit Las Vegas to soak up the atmosphere of the place. I was still under the age of twenty one so could not enter any of the amusement areas. On then to Sacramento Valley not then known as Silicone Valley, but more for its horticultural enterprises.

My main focus were the seed companies and I visited two seed compounds where I was made most welcome. I saw vegetables and flowers grown to a very high standard. Throughout my travels I met people who would give me contact details in the places I was planning to visit. This was another reason why planning was so important you didn't seem to be a stranger when you had friends in a town or city. My next stop was Portland which is probably best known for the imposing Mount Hood. Again, I met a friendly family here who showed me around. We went up to Timberlake Lodge on Mount Hood where there was a lot of skiing going on. It was a lovely clear day as the photograph that I took demonstrates so beautifully. After saying my goodbyes, my next destination was Seattle. I prepared myself the previous evening for an early start. In Seattle I had booked a hotel and then took a trip out to Port Angeles which involved a ferry ride. I discovered a nice place there with beautiful trees where I enjoyed a sandwich and a bit of a snooze! It was now the 19th May and only two days until my twenty first birthday which I hoped to spend in Vancouver with Pete and his friends. I did plenty in Seattle where there was a raised modern monorail to transport you around town. I visited the fairground, Volunteer Park and walked around the docklands and markets. I also visited the Science Centre and watched a film about Apollo 9 etc. After a most wonderful visit, it was time to depart for Vancouver.

It was quite difficult to get a seat on the bus because lots of people were flocking back to Canada to celebrate Queen Victoria's birthday. In many ways, the Canadians were more traditional in their celebrations than the people back home. All of these people travelling home caused quite a big jam at customs as we crossed the border. When I arrived in Vancouver, I was able to stay at Pete's flat and a friend of his came to pick me up from the bus station which was nice. I heard lots of Pete's news, his work and his travels since he had gone to Vancouver etc. I was pretty shattered so it was nice to chill out and relax for a while. It enabled me to catch up with washing my clothes and filling in my diary which has aided me immensely in this recount of my experiences in addition to the postcards that I sent to friends and family. That evening, Pete prepared some lovely salmon and we went out for a walk around English Bay. My birthday turned out to be a busy and exciting day. After opening some presents and making some phone calls I went downtown to the Tourist Information Office. I decided then to go to the well- known Stanley Park and it was lovely as my photos record; three white ducks waddling across a lawn in front of some lovely Rhododendrons in full bloom. I also went to a bridge on a river and ate beaver ha ha. When I returned, I phoned my mum back home and had a long chat with her. I then went out again to visit a planetarium and various museums. I came back rather late so had to rush to enjoy my twenty first celebrations which included a meal and a visit to the theatre where we saw 'Down The Greasy Pole', about an Italian community in New York. The following day I was off again on my travels and went to Vancouver Island. It was a lovely bus ride to Secuett with other, smaller islands and beautiful trees for which, British Columbia is well known. According to my diary, it appears that there were several ferries in the area to Powell River, Vancouver Island. To be honest, I cannot remember much about this. It appears that I spent quite a lot of time exploring, both day and night. I hitch hiked to Victoria and a few other places that I do not remember. The scenery was spectacular around Swartz peninsular and I stayed in a hotel since I'd been camping for the previous two nights, the equipment borrowed from Pete. It was nice to have really good wash and shave! It was very quiet in Victoria and I was able to enjoy the Parliament Buildings. After a good night's sleep, I went in search of the Tourist Information Office and ate a hearty breakfast of egg over, as they called it over there. I also needed to get my basic Kodak camera fixed because it had jammed. From Victoria I hitched a ride to the Bucharest Gardens in Brentwood Bay. The pelargoniums were very beautiful. From there I took another ferry to Tsucusson and it was very lovely going through the islands, then went on out to Richmond. All in all, it was a very successful excursion. By this time, it was 27th May and I had said my goodbyes to Pete. It would be a very long time before I saw him again and under very different circumstances.

I set out to New Westminster where I visited the Fraser family, friends of Pete. After this the bus took me through Roger's Pass and on to Banff and Lake Louise, high up in the Rockies. Here I stayed, in a hostel where I made friends with fellow travellers. I also visited Athabasca Glacier where people were enjoying rides on snowmobiles, onwards then to Banff. Banff is a very beautiful place at any time of the year and I visited the museum and learned about the local wildlife. I also visited and enjoyed, the hot springs as the snow lightly descended. A lovely sensation of hot and cold. This would, by no means, be the last time I would experience the springs but under very different circumstances. The following day, I hitched a ride to Lake Louise which, as my photos demonstrate, was a stunning and beautiful place. A contrast of colours- white snow, green trees and the deep blue of the lake and sky. After hitching back again, I caught a bus to Calgary. I didn't stop long there as I planned to come back later in the summer to the Stampede. There was a lot yet to happen between my first and second visits to Calgary. The bus then took us on to Edmonton, travelling across the Prairies which I found quite boringly flat! It was good that I found people to talk to and so pass the time. I visited Alberta game farm and, in the evening, I set out for Saskatoon. When I arrived, I ate breakfast and went out to the university campus as I was told that it was quite beautiful. Everything was nice apart from the midges at that time of the year. As a result, I couldn't do much relaxing outdoors. From there I went on to Winnipeg which I found quite disappointing and did not stay overnight. At 7pm I caught the bus to Port Arthur. Now, the landscape changed to a more wooded state, typical of Northern Ontario. I hitched to Kakabeka Falls which were very nice and from there I hitched to nearby Fort William. Then it was a bus to Loo St. Marie which is positioned at the top of the Great Lakes with lots of waterfalls. I took a pleasure cruise through the locks. After visiting friends, I was dropped off at the bus station for my next destination, Sudbury. The devastation to the environment due to the copper mining and processing was a sight to behold and truly shocking in a developed country. It was as though a nuclear bomb had been dropped on the area. There were hardly any green leaves and the trees were just bare skeletons. It was as though nobody cared about the damage that they were causing. When I visited the copper belt in Zambia some years later, I never witnessed the same level of devastation. I didn't stay long there but set off for Ottawa. I would, in later years, pass through Sudbury again...

When I arrived in Ottawa, I found a hotel where I washed and tidied myself up as I had spent quite a few nights on the bus. It was nice to be in the capital of Canada and it seemed to have a feeling of peace, tranquility and sophistication. Beautiful Parliament buildings sat alongside the concrete ones which seemed to blend quite well and they were also sympathetically landscaped. After visiting some friends, whose address I had been given, I set out for my return journey to Toronto and the Campbell's house. It was amazing that on my travels thus far that I had met so many lovely people, although I was very shy by nature. These friends and acquaintances developed into a sort of network. My next bus was to Boston via Niagara Falls. At that time, the America was virtually dry as they had diverted the river to restructure the crumbling cliffs. In Boston I visited some more historic sites and went to the State Capitol which was a most beautiful building especially inside where they also kept the archives in the basement. I then went on the 'Follow The Freedom Trail' to Durgin Park. From Boston, I went North to Portland, Bangor and then on to St Stephen, across the border back into Canada and then on to St John's in Nova Scotia. We passed over the Reversing Falls which we were able to view from the bus. In St John's, I had some lunch and then set off for Halifax, where I arrived at around 5pm. Next day, I visited friends and also did some sightseeing, visiting the Citadel. It appears that I have an insatiable appetite for sightseeing! The main thing that I remember about Halifax was the fog which made me feel quite at home. After this, I then went back inland to Lunenburg. I will always remember the black and white painted wooden church nestled in a glade of trees. From there I took the bus on to Portsmouth, Brunswick and then into New York. It was in New York where my luck finally ran out. I arrived in the early morning after a night on the bus getting some sleep as best I could. I fell asleep in the bus terminus and when I awoke, it was to discover that all of my luggage had been stolen. This consisted of perhaps two small bags. All that I had left was on my person. I had lost my passport but still had my traveller's cheques, my bus pass and around $50 in cash. The police were not going to help me much so I made my way to the British Consulate to get a temporary passport. I was fairly devastated but tried to put my tribulations behind me; perhaps New York was not such a bad place but I could not stay too long. I had to get back to Toronto to regroup. Firstly, I went to the Rockerfeller Centre and, of course, to the Empire State Building. I spent some time in Greenwich Village soaking up the atmosphere.

When I got to Toronto, the Campbells were away do I went to visit some friends. After visiting quite a few friends and re-organising myself I set off once again on the Greyhound bus to Detroit and on to Chicago. On my arrival in Chicago the weather was really nice and pleasant; cool, clear and sunny. My first impressions were good as I looked around the city. That evening, I visited friends who I had contacted earlier and spent a very nice evening socialising. The next day I visited several exhibitions and, in the evening, I took a bus deeper into Illinois and Nebraska. The scenery was rather flat and uninteresting. Of course, this was the prairie maize belt which used to be pasture for buffalo. The countryside gradually became more interesting as the bus passed through Wyoming and Cheyenne. Of course, this was typical cowboy country with romantic names such as Laramie etc which I had come to know through watching westerns on T.V. I then went down to Salt Lake City which, on the approach, showed me a lovely view of the city. The grey buildings against the blue sky made it appear quite a somber place. Then it was back on the bus again to West Yellowstone National Park on what happened to be, Independence Day. Things were really busy and made it easier to hitch hike through the park. Of course, I had to see Old Faithful and also some beautiful waterfalls and canyons. Afterwards, I hitched down through the Grand Tetons, then to Butte and on over the border to Calgary for the Stampede. For some strange reason, two things appeared to have run out at the same time which, to be honest, I wasn't really aware of. One was on around the 6th July, my bus pass ran out. The other was that I had virtually run out of money... The Stampede I didn't feel was impressive as I found it to be rather cruel, not unlike bull fighting. I cannot remember where I stayed but after two or three days, I decided it was time to head back to Toronto.

Again, my luck sort of ran out again but, in the end, turned out to be quite a memorable adventure! I had got myself onto the main highway, heading West out of town and tried to hitch a lift. There were at least twenty other travelers attempting to do the same thing so there was little chance of success for me. As I talked with some of the others, we realised the only way to head West was to jump the goods trains as a hobo. The police stopped and offered us a free night in a police cell where I slept on an old door which was gratefully accepted. In the morning, I got myself to the train tracks just out of town to catch the outgoing train. Earlier, I had been advised on how to jump the trains... You approach the train before it gathers too much speed (which is not rocket science...) You should choose where the engine is so as to keep warm, with the disadvantage that you get really sooty! I would throw my case onto the train, keeping my documents and the little money I had left, on my person in case I failed to get on. Of course, all of this is illegal and you needed to keep out of sight of the Railway Police, No safety in numbers so you did this on your own. On one occasion, I couldn't believe my luck when I jumped on a train carrying a cargo of brand new Chevrolet cars. I presumed they would be locked, but not at all. There I sat in all my glory in my brand new Chevrolet, one memorable experience of being a hobo for a few days. Of course, what I was doing was fraught with danger from all sorts of directions, injury, and the Railway Police being just two. The practice was to jump back off the train as it slowly entered a new town or city, walk around the train and catch another on the other side. I was given lots of advice as I travelled along. Much of the time it was very boring, going across the prairies again and, to be honest, I don't know how I got any sleep since I had to be very alert all of the time so as not to be found out. I suppose the noise of the engine would have helped to keep me awake. Upon arrival in Toronto, I had to be extra vigilant because it was the end of the lie and there were bound to be plenty of railway police about and so it proved to be. I saw someone who did get caught but, again, I was the lucky one. I was so obvious with my sooty body as I made my way to the Campbell's house. The first thing I did upon arrival was to have a good bath, tidy myself up, wash my dirty clothes and rest. I was virtually broke and needed some money to ay for a flight home. I think it was Mike's friend who found me a job picking cherries in the North of Toronto and I stayed in a very basic hut. Picking fruit was a very hot and sticky job. They were Morello cherries, of the type that are put on cocktail sticks in drinks. I'm not entirely sure how many weeks I was working there but I earned enough money to get a flight back home.

I arrived back home and was back to looking for work and, initially, living with my mum. I eventually found a job as an apprentice at Norcutts Nurseries and Garden Centre in Woodbridge, Suffolk, Not far from Ipswich. I was in lodgings which I did not enjoy much, the couple were not so friendly so I used to go to my mums at the weekend. I had virtually no social life although Woodbridge is a nice enough place. Initially I worked in the dispatch department where orders were assembled and transported out to the customers. Later, I was working in the container plant unit which kept me very busy. In the spring and summer, I worked in the garden centre stocking up the beds with plants as they were sold. I did not serve the customers. Once again, I could see myself progressing and settling but once again, I got itchy feet…

FURTHER STUDIES, WORK AND TRAVELS

It was off to Writtle again to study the Advanced Diploma in Horticulture with a view of trying to gain a National Diploma in Horticulture from the Royal Horticultural Society in Wisley, Surrey. This time around, I stayed on the campus but didn't enjoy the meals. So, on Fridays I would treat myself to fish and chips and a cool beer. I was made the house rep in my absence which did not please me, although it was not too arduous except when students got the fire hoses out and had water fights! I made good friends with Michael who had a diploma from Kew Gardens and had been looking after Richard Attenborough's garden. Michael said he was a very humble and kind man. I remember that I studied hard and callouses formed on my elbows which then became sore. I found the studies to be quite easy because I knew most of the lectures. Also, we were mature students who took the studies seriously and there was no messing around. Some of the students were married and had children. I had rather a strange method of studying. I would have a few hours until around 10.30 pm and then set about my studies until late into the night when all around was quiet. My studies went well and I gained the Advanced Diploma and also the NDH which was a real test of my abilities, both practically and theoretically. The practical exam was taken at Wisley and the examiners were watching you all of the time as you undertook the various tasks. This was quite nerve wracking, especially the surveying which I was not very good at and we were being examined by an examiner from Writtle who I think didn't like me and, consequently, I didn't like him either! I was pleasantly surprised when, after all my hard work, I gained a pass. For some long while, I had had an application form to do voluntary service overseas which I left on the windowsill at college. I was reluctant to fill it in due to my lack of confidence. Eventually I put pen to paper and submitted the application. I was pleasantly surprised when I was invited to go for an interview and was interviewed by quite a large panel. But all went well and I was accepted to eventually go to Zambia. Prior to that I attended an induction course at Reading University where we learned about the culture and a little about the language. Not being any good at languages, I did not progress much in this area. I had had this plan since I was at school when I had attended Geography classes and I had a very good teacher. This inspired me to travel and work abroad, firstly in North America and then in Africa. I was also able to travel a lot separately from this through my brother-in-law and also with my new wife when I married. I had plans to work in a developed country and then on to sample work in what we then called an underdeveloped country.

I journeyed home then to my mums one afternoon, from where, I'm not sure and it's not surprising since it's well over forty years ago now. All I remember is that I came to a roundabout at Weeley not so far from where my mum was living. I noticed two girls trying to hitch a lift at the side of the road. Having done a lot of hitch hiking myself, I had no hesitation in offering them a lift and was further motivated to do so because one of the girls had on a very short skirt! As I pulled up, a boy jumped out of the hedge but I was not phased. They told me they were from Czechoslovakia on an English Language course at Essex University. They said that they wanted to go to the seaside because they had never been before. Being a good diplomat, I suggested that they came to my mums for a cup of tea which they duly did. They took photos on the lawn, one of which I still have today. I then took them to Walton on the Naze, why I never went to Frinton I'll never know as it was much more pleasant there. After that, I took them back to Essex University and agreed to meet up one evening in a few days with one of the girls, Marta, who I found to be the most attractive. A few days later, I went to the university to collect her and took her into Colchester where we had a walk around and, I guess we had a few drinks. What I do remember is buying her a rather dull and boring tea pot which was a darkish blue with black markings. How she ever allowed me to buy it I'll never know! She was just too polite, I think. We still have that tea pot today although it's now a little battered. She is very good at keeping mementos as I do now and have come to appreciate. Anyway, how English and romantic was that gift?! I must have made a slight impression on her because she agreed to see me again the following weekend. We planned to meet at Liverpool Street Station after she had been to Cambridge with fellow students and tutors. It was a lovely place to go as I was later to appreciate. We went to my sister's flat in Cleveland Square. Now, bearing in mind that she was visiting the UK from a country under communism, they were very carefully watched, their passports were held by their tutors, she was taking a huge risk by staying with me for the weekend. In fact, some fellow students of hers did defect but I don't think that she considered it due to her strong family ties. I guess it must have been on a Saturday in the summer that I drove to London and met her off the train at Liverpool Street Station. In those days I did manage to drive in London but often got lost. I rarely drive in London today for the same reason. Anyway, we met up and I drove to my sister's flat and Marta shared a bedroom with my sister, I guess I slept on the lounge floor. She came from a completely different background but we seemed to hit it off very well. She was five years younger than me and had just graduated. That evening, we went to the theatre and saw a lovely amusing play called, 'There's a Girl in my Soup!' The next day we decided that it would be nice to visit Kew Gardens. I had visited before as part of my horticultural studies and I knew it would be a nice day but just not how nice... It must have been one of those special places to have a romantic encounter; at least it was for me. The beautiful trees, the palm house with the great indoor water lilies. It was one of those very special days and I believe it cemented our relationship which was going to take some years to come to its fruition. To be brief, we did walk around and look at a few plants but most of the time we sat on a bench and were in one another's arms and being very amorous! She told me later that her mother had told her that if a girl kisses a boy too much, she can become pregnant I took her back early to Colchester where she received quite a scolding as she was later to tell me. Although if she had asked permission to be with me, they probably wouldn't have allowed it. It was not long after that when her course ended and it was time for her to go back to Bratislava. I had just one more visit to the university where I was invited to a leaving party. For most of the evening she chose to sort of ignore me and, as I later learned, she was spoilt for choice with the large number of boys that were interested in her. She was an attractive young woman with a warm character and a quiet sense of humour but a determined individual as I was later to learn. I also learned later that she was also interested in a French boy. Otherwise, I only remember two things… I got quite upset and cried when we said goodbye because I never expected to see her again. The other was that we agreed to write to each other and she gave me a black and white passport sized photo of herself which was attractive and I still have it to this day. I drove back to mums feeling rather sad as I had grown to love her very much although I hardly knew her! I knew that, of course, I could not make any commitment as I would shortly be leaving for Zambia and she had hinted that she had promised herself to someone back at home. For now, it was time to make my preparations for Zambia.

At the induction at Reading University, most were younger than me, just having graduated from university. I wrote one or two letters to Marta and received at least one brief reply before I left for Zambia. Once there, I was given a project in Lusaka in what was called the Makeni Ecumenical Centre where they were setting up a training scheme to settle squatters as small holders just outside Lusaka so they could supply to the city markets. It was run by a South African priest and his Dutch brother. The other projects included a clinic, nutrition centre, shop, cookery, women's groups and classes on malnutrition and family planning etc. I was to be an instructor alongside a chap from Southern Rhodesia who had spent time in South Africa as a supporter of the ANC. We also had a Zambian instructor, the first one we had was an alcoholic and so had to be dismissed. My fellow instructor (who was married) and I, were give brand new accommodation on site and we had a large bedroom each with a shared shower room and kitchen. When socialising or having a meal, we would sit out on the veranda and enjoy the fresh air. The couple I shared with had got to know one another at Nottingham University and she taught at the local Zambian school called Matero. We three became great friends and we got on well together, she would do most of the cooking so once again I was spoilt. I think it was the first Sunday that I was there that I was asked by Pierre, the boss to read the lesson in the church service. This I politely declined, not wanting to be the new white boy in town taking over the show. I think my decision was not appreciated. One amazing thing about the accommodation, I noticed that as I closed my eyes when I took a shower, as one does, there appeared to be flashes across my eyes. I couldn't understand why but reported it to Pierre anyway. Knowing a little about electricity, he immediately knew what the problem was, the electrician had connected the earth to the water supply! I am lucky to be alive! Another experience that was not quite so dangerous… I was on my own one weekend and went out to look at the student's plots when there was a strike of lightning directly overhead and the thunder was unrelenting and scary. I went quickly to the accommodation in pure fright, running for my life.

In the beginning we went out to the local squatter townships to recruit potential trainees. We got them to submit written applications and then we held interviews. The first group we had consisted of about wenty and it was easy for them to do the first task, making an African hoe. This hoe had to be able to carry out such tasks as cultivating, digging, trenching and of course, weeding. The handle would be made of local wood. As it was a new project, the next job was to install security fencing. We were in the suburbs od Lusaka where things could easily go missing. After that they were allocated individual plots where they were able to construct raised beds of around ten in number, two metres wide and a one metre wide path, each approximately ten metres long. This enabled them to have an extra depth of topsoil to which compost could be added. Depending on the season, they could grow all manner of crops including lettuce, tomatoes, peppers, aubergines, cabbage and rape (a leaf vegetable similar to kale) sweet potatoes and grape nuts etc. We also taught formal lessons where they were able to learn about crop rotation, conservation, nutrition, varieties of crops, pest and diseases, poultry keeping, marketing and finance. No doubt I have left something out!

Piped water was from a borehole as watering was needed during the extended dry season which was about six months long. One of my main passions was to produce compost to aid the soil fertility. This was very easy in the hot climate and made easier by having poultry manure to ensure the heap heated up easily and contained plenty of nitrogen. We would make a compost above ground and used eucalyptus sticks with chicken wire mesh to contain the compost. In that climate it was not necessary to thin the compost so we were able to produce it in a matter of months as opposed to at home where it took a year or so. The compost bins were one and a half metres high and two metres square. We alternated the poultry manure with layers of weeds, vegetable waste, grass and maize waste to improve aeration and speed up the composting process. I loved all of this as opposed to the formal classes as I was not good at standing up and spouting forth! I still lacked confidence unlike my colleague who was in his element. Keeping poultry, I had never done before, not at that level and in that climate. It was not so technical but I still struggled with the chicks and was not very popular with the boss as quite a few of them died because I was not keeping them warm enough. Plants are more my thing! In that sub Saharan climate, keeping chickens well and also well ventilated was the priority. So, we constructed the chicken houses with a short breeze block wall and a corrugated tin roof supported by eucalyptus poles. Chicken wire was then fixed from the wall to the roof to keep out vermin. Our boss knew a lot about chickens and he kept them for home consumption. I think he thought of me as a bit useless and inept. It surprised me, even in that climate, how warm the chicks need to be kept and, of course, any water spilt means death to them. A couple of other things enter my head from my time staying at Makeni, one of which was the lightning experience. The other was that I noticed that the locals used to pick leaves for spinach from a particular weed that they called Chibondwe and was found on waste ground. I decided to gather some seeds which were plentiful. I would then grow these so called weeds on cultivated compost soil so the crop was quite bountiful and made more succulent and productive.

As time went on, a sort of mistrust seemed to build up between the trainees, the bosses and us instructors. With hindsight, I realise why. They began to think that they were being use as cheap labour and they could not see the benefits of their work. There were some historic reasons regarding their feelings with particular reference to the period of colonization and we were four white guys instructing and bossing black Africans. After several months, they went on strike and the atmosphere became pretty unpleasant. I know that I was devastated and pretty confused as to what to do about the matter and just how it would all be resolved. But that trust had gone for the remainder of my stay there. Most of the trainees were Bemba and the remainder, Lozi from the Western Province and Tonga from the Southern province who were the ones most adept at growing crops. One Tonga man I remember was Samson Maambo who was a big and thoughtful gentleman. So, when it came to the dispute, he was a type of peacemaker and I could feel his sense of frustration at what was going on. For me perhaps, being still rather immature, the project seemed to lose its way and I was certainly out of my depth. What made matters worse was that Ben, the other white instructor, decided to leave because he was not happy at the way things were going. That left me feeling rather lonely and vulnerable. I decided that it would be best if I also made a move.

Still with the VSO, I approached the British Consul, or they came to me, I cannot remember if they had come to hear of my plight. Either way, a lovely lady, Catherine, was very sympathetic to my situation and found a job for me in Southern Province with the Tonga. Before I go on to relate my experiences on the family farms, I must track back to my time at Makeni to a couple of things that I have neglected to mention but were pleasant and memorable experiences... Although it is called 'Voluntary Service Overseas', it is, in fact, not voluntary as we received local wage rates which were more than adequate because I stayed at the project rent-free. The cost of food was cheap and I was given a small motorbike through VSO which allowed me to go on two or three holidays. The first of which was to Malawi with three or four fellow volunteers, in fact, Lake Malawi was our destination. We of course hitchhiked and I have a picture of us sunbathing on the back of a lorry! Lake Malawi was like a paradise for me. Although not a keen swimmer, going in the freshwater lake was like swimming in an aquarium. It was crystal clear so you could observe the tropical, brightly coloured fish at close quarters. The other trip was with my sister who came to visit. The first was to Luangwa National park which, for me, was a life-long experience. We flew in and stayed in Rondavels and were treated like royalty. When we were not viewing big 'game' we were lounging by the pool and observing elephants going through the danbo- a wet, marshy area. The final trip was to South Africa via Southern Rhodesia. Once again we hitch hiked through Victoria Falls or Mosi-oa-Tunya which means 'The Mist That Thunders'. We got a lift with an overt racist who was most unpleasant but, we were in his car so had to keep 'schtum'! In South Africa we visited a family friend in Durban and I particularly remember a day when there was a demonstration by a local African on how to make compost. This he did below ground. He was much admired by everyone, even the white ladies at that time of Apartheid. From there we went to Port Elizabeth to enjoy the Indian Ocean. Then, it was back to Lusaka and goodbye to my sister.

Now back to Family Farms... This turned out, for me, to be one of the most challenging yet positive experiences of my life to date, as it came with a lot of responsibility. It tested my skills to the utmost but I have always enjoyed a challenge. Prior to myself starting on a new settlement, I helped out at a neighbouring settlement, because for legal and other reasons, my settlement was not ready to take. I should explain the basics of the project...It is to settlement vacant land using European farms with competent local farms. Prior to me starting, there were five or six other settlements with a white advisor and a Zambian assistant, the latter would take over when settlement had taken place. The whole concept had been initiated by a Canadian volunteer who had amazing foresight. So, prior to starting I could feed off their experiences. I was given an amazingly large area to settle, about 22,000 acres or approximately five miles by nine miles. The area was suitably large because most of it was rocky bush and quite infertile so only useful for extensive grazing. So, to create usable areas, they had to be large in size and with fencing. The Tonga are well known for their cattle keeping. Each farm had to be 500 acres or more to support the family enterprise, hence they were known as family farms. The farm would consist of the farmer, usually with more than one wife, the extended family plus workers, so it was like a small village. To help us settlement advisors, we had Zambian assistants to create continuity. He would already have been a successful agricultural advisor in the native area and would be seconded to family farms by the government. So, assisting on the neighbouring settlement was a useful lead in and allowed me to make my preparations regarding accommodation etc. I first stayed in a rather luxurious ex European's farmhouse with nice gardens, running water, electricity and telephone etc. After a short while I was allocated an assistant named Enoch who himself, was a bit of a character, as I was to discover. He was quite small but had plenty of energy and his favourite music was Jim Reeves. I found him a very easy person to get along with as he was very diligent, respected and had a nice sense of humour. There was not a bad word between us over the three or four years that I worked with him. At the time, he had one wife and one child. So, there were a few plans we had to put in place before the settlement could get underway. I would live with Enoch on this Silwili settlement, as it was called, owing to a large hill in the area called Silwili. The whole Area consisted of two European farms plus some other government land. The two European farms were owned by one European farmer who had three African wives, two on the farms and one in the town of Monze, as I was led to understand. He had a house to each wife so told Enoch to have one with his wife and I was to have the other. I decided, being single, to take the more remote house which also required quite a lot of work to be done on it. So, I could stay back on Kazangula, the neighbouring settlement, while the work was carried out. The other house was in good condition and was near the main road so Enoch and his family could move in there straight away.

The house I was to move into was just a shell as the corrugated roof had to be removed and the frames as well. Also, a lot of the timber had been eaten away by termites. Soon after I arrived, I started to visit the local bars and having a bit of a social life. This was going to get me into some serious trouble as I will relate at a later point. I have always had a strange relationship with alcohol as the experience whilst still at school (as I recounted earlier) proves... I also conducted my business increasingly in pubs and bars. There, in Penba, a nearby town, I met a man, Miles Mutanga who ran a local building business. I negotiated with him to do the renovation work on the house which as I've said, was remote and about five miles from any road and about five or six miles from the main tarmac road to Livingston going South and Lusaka to the North. My bath water had to be heated by an out drain over a wood fire which was fed from a borehole which, in turn, filled a concrete tank by way of a foot pump as there was no electricity. I used a paraffin fridge to keep my persishable food. I also organised accommodation for a servant and his family to help with things around the place. No huge tasks, but it gave someone employment and made life easier for me as I was really busy. There was no chance of having any sort of garden because the soil was so infertile.

Initially, the things I had to do with Enoch was to get the settlement scheme up and running. There were many tasks involved and one was to write applications for farmers from the native areas within the region, the other was to have the whole settlement area soil surveyed so it could be assessed as to its agricultural value. We also needed to assess water supplies. It was a matter of matching the farmer's capabilities to the land that we had. It would have to be 500 Acres, or more, in size to support the family enterprise, hence the name, 'family farms.' Enoch and I had small Honda motorbikes to do our visits to farmers etc. In the warm climate, it was lovely to ride around without helmets on. The law did not insist on helmets at that time. Just to feel the wind through my hair was very refreshing. We also used our motorbikes for socialising and shopping. I had a cool box on the back of mine for when I shopped for perishable items. Sometimes we would need a pick-up truck to carry materials and to use as a taxi, common in those parts. We borrowed that when necessary from neighbouring settlements. I also taught Enoch and the neighbouring advisor, Jack, how to drive, so they could be more independent.

In order for the selection of farmers to be as democratic as possible, it was perhaps best for an outsider, such as myself, to do the selection, obviously with advice from my assistant, Enoch. To aid with this there was also a settlement committee chaired by the local governor to try and improve the transparency. Fortunately, he turned out to be very conscientious and a thorough man in his dealings with us. This made our jobs a lot easier but, on the other hand, being a politician, he was quite tough to deal with. This was particularly the case with the squatters as it was quite a contentious issue and nobody wanted to evict anyone! Some had considerable investment in their villages etc and where would they go once evicted? It was a pleasurable experience visiting the farmers over such a wide area which gave me a sense of freedom. Almost without exception, we were made very welcome. Only with squatters, were we treated with suspicion and this was fair enough.

Invariably, before any serious discussions started, we would be offered some refreshments or a meal. We have to remember, in no way were these people rich but they were happy to share what little they had with us, always with a smile. The best meal I had there was a very simple breakfast. It consisted of maize kernels soaked in water for a day or so until the starches turned to sugar. To this was added soured milk from their cattle and a little sugar. Delicious!! The squatters were the most difficult to assess, partly because they might not always get on with their neighbours having left the native areas. They could be people who were difficult to integrate into the settlement system but, I think we were understanding regarding their predicament. These people were the most difficult to decide on.

As is common in most parts of Africa, rural society revolved around growing staple crops and keeping animals. In the case of the Tonga, it was cattle, which gave them prestige, particularly when it came to the price of a bride. In general, the condition of the animals was not of prime importance but more the number of cattle. This led to a difficult dilemma, particularly in times of drought, whether to sell the cattle or not. In times of drought the cattle would be thin and so not fetch the best price. As the farmers become wealthier, they change to a more commercial outlook regarding their cattle. Changing the outlook of the farmers is a long objective if not only to avoid soil erosion and the deterioration of pastures through over grazing. Especially since in that area, the soil is so poor in the first place. I think the attitude of my generation needs to truly change. After intensive visits to these farmers, some as many as three or four visits, we were in a position to assess their suitability for the land we had available. A short list was drawn up and the three main criteria were; the amount of available land required, the amount and quality of grazing, the water supply and lastly, any farming specialities such as vegetable or fruit growing and the keeping of any livestock such as pigs and chickens .Some of the farmers would be allocated over a thousand acres as the grazing was so poor in parts. This was a heavy investment for them in terms of time and money to erect fencing on their boundaries. We had to carefully balance boundary responsibilities to avoid disputes. It was particularly difficult with the larger farms because fencing such long lengths over such harsh terrain was obviously demanding with regard to expense etc.

During this time, I had my own accommodation to sort out with Miles. In general, he was quite efficient and diligent but, because of the state of the building, the work still took several weeks. Eventually, the time arrived when we had to submit the farmer's names to the committee chaired by the local governor, I guess he would be comparable to a Mayor in our towns. There were also other interested parties on the committee, mostly in the agricultural field. Other local charities and workers in the health field were also on the committee. Because the governor was a political figure, he would want to please the local population and do the best for them. In this way he would gain votes when it came to the local elections so he would question very carefully about the squatters that we wanted to evict. I could see his point of view because our primary purpose was to assess the candidates according to their suitability to the land that we had available. It was not dissimilar to trying to juggle ten balls and keep them all up in the air at the same time! In the end, there would be a satisfactory meeting of minds and we selected around twenty five farmers in order for them to become self-sufficient and hopefully prosper.

One of the problems we had was that some of the farmers came from an area which had contagious diseases amongst their cattle. The cattle were given the appropriate medical treatment and transported by truck into the new settlement area in the hope of avoiding further contamination. This was all paid for by the local agricultural department. Other than helping the farmers to settle, our other main task was to survey and set the boundaries, an arduous task due to the rocky terrain and dense bush. This had to be done carefully in order to avoid future disputes. I had to spend many hours in the evening, by candlelight, preparing the boundaries to agreed specifications and working out the co-ordinates. This was a chore that did not come naturally to me. I also had to decide which boundaries had to be fenced by which farmers and, as far as possible, the responsibilities were shared equally between them. Once the farms had been allocated, and all of the boundaries agreed, a proper surveyor was employed by the agricultural department. In some areas it was said that there was wild buffalo, a really dangerous animal when confronted, however, we never came across any.

Although it was lovely to live in this remote area, I decided that I needed to eat more healthily to avoid becoming ill. It was quite easy to pick up bugs especially the 'runs' which I caught, fortunately only once and was quite unpleasant but not nearly as bad as when I visited another part of Africa at a later date. I rode down to a local small town on my motorbike, cool box on the back, where there were a number of good shops, mostly

Greek owned. I could buy local meat, vegetables and fruit. I would often buy a T-bone steak once a week as a special treat. I was naturally reared and hung so was always sweet and tender. I also made a good attempt to make marmalade but it was too runny, I had not realised that I needed pectin...

Although I had a servant, I did not expect him to cook for me. He did not have much to do as the soil was so poor, it was not worth having any sort of garden. The only thing we had were some local chickens so we got occasional eggs when we could find them. I also kept a local breed dog. Mostly, Enoch did cleaning, washing and ironing and it was nice to have him nearby and not feel too lonely. As I have previously mentioned, my social life was not good. I began to visit the local bars, particularly one small town, Pelusa, where one or two of the bars had a juke box. I could pick my meal up in the same town. Zambia, like many countries, has a fondness for various beers both bottled and local brews. It was the custom of the locals (even the women!) to open the bottle tops with their teeth- not for me!! Traditionally, they made their beer from maize kept in a forty gallon drum for around seven days until it ferments, dependent upon the time of year. The end result was a drink rather like a runny porridge and was drunk communally, passing around a large plastic container. Sometimes, I did return home rather intoxicated! One night I was really quite drunk and I was trying to be especially careful a s I crossed a dried up stream, about a mile from my house, on my motorbike. Unfortunately, I hit a large rock, lost my balance and fell off. My wrist caught between the handlebar and the brake lever, it was obviously broken and looked like a humped back bridge! I managed to struggle, along with my bike, back to the house, no doubt swearing all the way. I had no other transport and had to suffer for most of the night, taking numerous Dispirins to ease the pain. In the morning, John, my servant, got news out about my problem to the locals at a nearby settlement and so got me to a local hospital. I was operated on and put in plaster. That put an end to visits to the bars for a while but at the first opportunity I was back on a regular basis. However, I did not learn from this experience as I will recount later...

Eventually, I did meet a girl, Flora, who went on to become my girlfriend. She, like me, enjoyed a drink and we spent far too much time in the two bars that we used to frequent. It was one of the few ways that I could unwind, otherwise, there was not a lot else to do. I did visit some nearby Irish Jesuit missionaries where we played cards and it was nice relaxing with them and their easy-going sense of humour. They were also good, humble people. One fear I did have came about because of the death of a fellow VSO that I had heard about, although I had never met him. He was on his motorbike, saw a snake in the middle of the road, panicked and, unfortunately, fell off his bike, the snake bit him on the head and he passed away. His parents must have been devastated. Nothing like that ever happened to me although I had seen a few snakes, mainly Puff Adders in the rivers and lakes. When I got back, any type of snake on the road would frighten me. Whilst on the settlement I made a few visits to other areas. One was to Lake Kariba where I visited a Dutch couple who were doing a development under the hot and oppressive conditions of the Gwembe valley. When I arrived, my friend was not at home but his wife told me that he was down by the dam, at the lakeside, skinning a dead crocodile. It had been dead for a few days and was pretty foul smelling and bloated. However, he was determined to skin it as, I guess, when cured, it would be quite valuable. It was there that I suspect I became infected with bilharzia, more of that later...

On perhaps more than one occasion we took a trip to Kafue National Park with its vast expanse of prairie-like landscape. There were no crops but plenty of Gazelles to view. The rivers at that time were teeming with fish, mostly a variety which the locals called Kapenta, a very small silver fish. Lovely cooked fresh but it can also be salted and dried, available throughout the year and very nutritional for those living in the towns and cities. Part way through my time at Family Farms, my two year contract with VSO was coming to an end so I signed on for another eighteen months in order to complete the work on the settlement scheme. This allowed me to make my first trip back home.

I cannot remember much of what I did other than spend quite a lot of time in hospital, not that I was really unwell. The first time was for a two or three day visit to the hospital for Medical and Tropical Diseases to have some tests for bilharzia which luckily proved negative as I had rejected the organism. It became quite interesting as I was able to share travel stories with my fellow patients. The next visit was to Bart's hospital where my kind sister had booked me in for tests about some strange symptoms. These were probably caused by some sort of food poisoning because of some out of date sausages that I had eaten. Not advisable at all but especially not in the Tropics! None of the tests came back positive and gradually the symptoms went away. It was a lovely experience being in these traditional wards with a matron in her lovely blue uniform who happened to be a friend of my sister. Who ever said they liked being in hospital?! But I was royally treated.

When I went back to Family Farms it was a matter of completing things at the settlement and preparing Enoch, as far as possible, to take over. There was quite a good support network in Family Farms with a very helpful financial advisor who guided us regarding our finances and how to keep our book work up to date. We he had regular meetings with fellow advisors and their assistants and learnt through their experiences and, of course, we had a good leader to guide us. There was also a bore hole section available to farmers if they could afford it. It was subsidised and, of course, loans were available in suitable cases. These were arranged through the local banks. Some settlements spent quite a lot of money on local improvements to include bridges, causeways and general drainage and the dirt roads needed regular maintenance. Although this was necessary as the area was extensive and there were a number of public roads running through the settlements which were also bordered by the new tarmac road. All of these experiences were generally positive and it was a most rewarding period of my life at this relatively young age. Only two difficulties arose and they were easily overcome. One was that my first assistant was an alcoholic and was replaced by Enoch. The second was, I found, rather funny! Unfortunately, one day, Enoch decided to go to a rather dangerous place, the bed of the wife of one of the neighbouring settlement farmers. His name was Joseph and he had been the manager to the previous European farmer. He had a good work ethic and so, was an ideal farmer to settle. However, if you were to ever meet Joseph you would be shocked by his impressive size, not unlike Goliath. For example, he had huge hands, more than three times the size of my own but he was a gentle giant. It is said that as Enoch was enjoying himself with Joseph's wife, Joseph arrived home. The story went that as soon as Enoch heard Joseph's voice he literally flew through the window (it had no glass) and ran away as fast as he could. As far as I knew then, there was no retaliation but I guess Enoch never went back there again! I never spoke with Enoch about all of this as it was none of my business and, of course, it was all hearsay.

When it came to the sad time to leave for home, I felt that it was only fit and proper that I should have a leaving party. This turned out to be a two day and two night event as was my habit. Since I had moved into the house, I had acquired a small flock of chickens and they gradually increased in number because they ran wild and their eggs were not always easy to find. At the time of the party, all of the chickens were killed by John. We also purchased a young pig which a fellow VSO slaughtered and it was spit roasted and we had plenty of rice, vegetables and some nzimi (a local maize meal) with it. A lovely feast! The accompanying local ladies brewed up a forty gallon drum of local beer and we also had quite a few crates of bottled beers and soft drinks. Of course, Flora, my girlfriend, was one of the organisers and one of the revelers too. We were a long way from any village so there was no problem with any noise nuisance regarding our music. Of course, I had mixed emotions but enjoyed the party with its African music. Any clothes I did not need I gave to Flora and friends as it seemed the least that I could do. I made plans to visit various countries in Africa on my way home, that I had never visited before. They included Cameroon, Nigeria, Sierra Leone and finally, Casablanca in Morocco. The leaving is always a lasting memory but I had a lot of fun up until the last.

When I think about my homeward bound trip, it was perhaps, a little disappointing due to the hot and oppressive climate in those parts and there was not so much of interest for me to see. Maybe, with hindsight, that judgement is not really fair, I did not venture far outside the main cities. However, it was an interesting experience, especially when my hotel room was broken into in Freetown. Something that sometimes seems to be my luck, someone brought back the things that had been stolen. What I did not fully realise is that I was not very well and this gradually became apparent. I had initially put it down to the heat but by the time I got to Freetown I realised that I had hepatitis as my urine and eyes were yellow. I decided to hurry home and, in the end, I didn't even leave the airport in Casablanca. I just boarded the next available flight back home. Another reason that I did not want to delay getting home was that my sister was about to be married and I was due to 'give her away' to an acquaintance of mine, more of that later... However, there was no way that I was well enough to give my sister away or to even attend her wedding. All I wanted to do was rest so I spent the day in bed instead. The reception was held in our mum's house as I rested upstairs. In the event, my sister was given away by her friend, a talented surgeon who had a practice at a London clinic on Harley Street. Her boss, John Griffiths came up to visit me and gave me some really useful advice, for which I am grateful to this day and extremely pleased that I followed his advice. He advised me not to drink any alcohol for at least six months as I could cause permanent damage to my liver. He told me to look into his eyes and I could see that they were a little yellow, as was his face. He had not observed the six months rule…

Upon my arrival back home, I knew it was time to make some important decisions about my future as I was now approaching twenty five or six years old. Of course, as I convalesced, I had plenty of time to think about it. I was at some sort of a crossroads in my life regarding my career. I also realised that if I was to set some sort of a goal for myself, I could not follow in my father's footsteps as vegetables were very difficult to make a profit out of. Additionally, I did not want to forge my career out of development work as my brother did because I don't like moving around so much. I liked being in England. I did not have a partner or even a girlfriend and I guessed that might not be so easy if I was abroad. I had a hankering to start my own business to give me independence and to challenge my capabilities. I was not ready to embark on that at that time, I needed to do some research. I gradually set about finding myself a job and began to read the advertisements in the Gardener's Chronicle. It took the best part of six months to recover from the hepatitis as I think it does most people. You certainly feel very lethargic for a good few months. However, as I recovered, I was able to stay with my friend, Pete and his family, who I knew from college and my Canada days. At this time, he and his father were operating a 'pick your own' enterprise and I was able to help them out and regain my strength. Being outdoors and eating well certainly aided my slow recovery.

BACK HOME, WORK AND BUSINESS

I continued to check the Gardener's Chronicle and made a few written applications. After one or two interviews, I was invited to an interview in the new city of Milton Keynes. I had a bit of a 'banger' of a car and managed to get myself quite lost on the way there and arrived about half an hour late. This turned out to be no problem because the gentleman who interviewed me was very relaxed and told me that most people arrived late because the roads were not well sign posted. We chatted about my work experience and he explained the concept of the new city. He had already worked in Hemel Hampstead which was an earlier new town. One of its other names was 'The City of Trees' which is what attracted me to the place. I was fortunately offered the job of landscaper, the position was previously known as 'the clerk of works.' I willingly accepted the job as I could see the potential of the place and it would be useful to develop my career. I found some basic accommodation after spending some time in a grotty bed and breakfast. It was a short distance from the Open University and I joined the film club to take up one evening of the week. At the start of my new employment, I was not kept very busy because the central area for which I was responsible was still being built or only at the planning stage. However, I assisted my new colleagues with the other areas, North and South. Some days I had so little to do so I went home and did some work on my small garden. I am someone who needs to be kept busy. Soon, my old car became unreliable and I got myself a reasonable loan from Milton Keynes Development Corporation (MKDC) and bought myself a new Triumph Spitfire in yellow. It was probably not my best decision because I was visiting buildings where there were various machines around and the roads were very muddy.

As time went by, being in a relatively new organisation, I managed to carry out my job through my own persistence and tried to innovate new ideas with the help of others. I was met with resistance to some of these ideas but eventually they bore fruit. I found some of the practices around horticultural principals and procedures, developed by the landscape architects, did not measure up with regard to plant requirements and the grass seed mixtures being used. The architects were good at their desks but not so clever at knowing what the plants needed such as soil type etc. Additionally, the soil conditions were not easy as it was mostly heavy clay, more suited to brick making and not much else other than low grade grassing. This was partly the reason why the area was initially chosen as it did not have much agricultural value. As a consequence, plants chosen by the landscape architects did not necessarily suit the prevailing soil conditions, they would perform poorly and there could be substantial losses. This was all exaggerated by poor horticultural practices and maintenance. Even simple matters such as grass seed mixtures were inappropriate and the grassed areas were not healthy and lacked vigour, they didn't wear well. Eventually, a landscape architect was asked to research the area and new seed mixes were introduced. A lot of basic research had to be done which all took a lot of time. After a while, it was decided to bring in the new chief landscape architect who had worked in the area for some time and this, in turn, enabled change to move forward in many areas. The year that I arrived, 1976, was a summer of prolonged drought resulting in a lot of plant losses. This was the responsibility of the contractors but some relief was given. When I started work in August/September, my main job was to help my two colleagues to count the plant losses which was done with a representative of the contractor. Because there was a drought, plant losses were more usual but they had to be replaced at the contractor's expense and quite a few aspects made this situation worse. Soil preparation was very basic, using farmyard manure that introduced weeds, weeding and general maintenance was poor, mulches were rarely used and little or no watering was the norm. All of this made it difficult for the contractors to get sites into a suitable condition in order to hand back to MKDC

. I also became involved in the construction of play areas, playing fields and the specialist areas such as indoor planting. Because I was involved in the central area with its adjoining housing estates it meant planting up the boulevards with Plane trees. There were also indoor plants in the shopping area and in some of the adjoining offices which had their own special needs and challenges. As time went by, my workload increased which was good as I liked to be kept busy. There were quite a lot of heated discussions about various landscape issues, some of which I had success with and others when I had to back down. With such large projects there is always bound to be clashes of personalities. One of the main issues, as far as I was concerned, was to get a clear depth of topsoil in the planting areas and also to have properly drained and top soiled tree pits, particularly in hard areas. The builders, in the beginning, did not even excavate the planting areas and, even worse, just buried building debris and covered it with a sprinkling of topsoil so that it looked okay. When they had done this there were pieces of brick, concrete, rubble and wood in these planting areas. After some time and quite a lot of arguing, I was allowed to check the depth of the topsoil prior to the completion certificate being signed. By doing this, I'm sure that I was intruding into someone else's responsibilities. The building architects designed the courtyards with sharp corners which made it difficult or impossible to cut the grass. Some time later, and at further expense, these courtyards were re-shaped and top-soiled which made the area softer and easier to maintain.

The building architects were very regimental in their approach to design. I remember on one occasion, going around with an architect and I could not believe it when he said it was a pity that residents would be moving in because they would all have different coloured curtains! In fact, the flats all had flat roofs and beige bricks and some cladding (which caused a lot of difficulties in the future) particularly as the builders on one estate allowed debris to fall into the cavity walls. Additionally, when stripping the topsoil prior to the building work getting underway, there was little management as to how the topsoil was handled and protected. I believe that some of the soil was being used or sold outside the city. Eventually we began to have proper soil surveys, done usually by myself and topsoil stockpiles were to be only three metres high and kept free of weeds. The excess soil was taken to stockpiles scattered throughout several locations in the city. Later on, we also did this with limestone rock to make rockeries etc and enlarge the landscaped areas at no great cost.

The biggest project for the area was the shopping centre consisting of two long malls of approximately one kilometre and an East/West orientation. This was ideal for a variety of planting, hot and cool. The mall's walls were paneled with warm beige marble with seats surrounding the planting holes. One of these was planted with temperate and sub-tropical plants including palms, cacti dracaena, eucalyptus and many more species besides. The architects had designed the building to be heated by hot air curtains as there would be no doors and so, open to the elements. The shutters would also help to keep the malls warm but at the time of planting, none of the malls were occupied. The building was at the highest point in the city and in midwinter was very exposed to a cold East wind. The air curtains could not stop the frosty winds because the building acted as a sort of wind tunnel. In the end, it was not just hard for the plants but also for the staff in the shops, particularly those who were on the tills because they were near the exits. It was so bad that they had to wear coats to keep warm and, of course, everyone's heating bills must have been astronomical! It was not going to help the plants much either. As the new boy on the block and working with some quite strong architects, it wasn't easy and

I had to back down but feared the outcome. I had expressed my opinion but it was not listened to. Work like that, as with many big projects, was running behind schedule but the plants had been ordered with the contractor. It was decided to take delivery of the plants and go ahead with the planting in late autumn or early winter. In the event this was all done in advance of the shops opening meaning that we had no heat from the units. When the winter came there was a very cold wind blowing through the building and we tried to protect the plants with hessian fleece and a thick polythene wall, but to no avail.

On the boulevards we also had problems with the Plane trees. They had been grown in MKDC nurseries in Milton Keynes village where the soil is good, light and fertile. Several thousand of these trees were growing in the nursery and were to be used mainly on the boulevards in the city centre. This was to give a nice urban feel as the trees matured. The problem was that due to work being generally behind schedule, the trees had grown too big to be transplanted, either bare root or root balled. In order to maintain the trees, they had to be undercut to reduce the root spread and, using a platform the heads were pruned to reduce them and I had to supervise all of this work. I was also involved with liaising regarding the planting of these trees. One of the most amazing aspects, when it came to the planting of the trees, was that the road engineers were obsessed, to almost a millimetre, that the trees were in a perfectly straight line! They did not realise that when a tree had a diameter of 300mm or more, it would have no significance. It is nice to see these trees now and I liken them to elephants as they mature. A lasting legacy for the future with this and all of the other planting, as Capability Brown did for us.

Eventually electric doors were fitted to the shopping centre at even more expense, replanting had to take place and eventually things settled down. Of course, it was not an easy scheme to maintain, the shoppers have to be considered with regard to health and safety. When it came to using chemicals to curtail pests and diseases, we decided to go for the organic environmentally friendly option, using parasites etc that had proved successful in the past. Of course, over the years, the planting has been adjusted and adapted to lend a softness to a rather plain and austere building. As I have already mentioned, there is very little good soil in Milton Keynes, so, for special projects such as the shopping centre, we sought supplies from outside the city. This was put out to tender and worked well. On one occasion, I noticed that where the Ampthill bypass was being constructed, it went through a rich peaty area which was being removed from the site and, presumably, sold. I contacted the contractor and we had some brought into Milton Keynes. After all of this preparation and planning we were never short of soil. As if we didn't have enough problems, we also had a problem with irrigation which was reasonably easily overcome. The specification that the subcontractors chose was not fit for purpose. It consisted of a pump room with electronics to water the beds in sequence. The problem arose with the plastic perforated pipes that were installed 150mm below the seats. When there was a blockage or system malfunction, it would not be discovered until the plants started to wilt, then it was difficult to access the pipes to repair them. Later, a drip system was installed which meant that we didn't need to hand water and so saved time and labour.

When I had been in Milton Keynes for a few months, I certainly thought that I could spend a few years in the area. I was now twenty eight years old and was in a position to buy my first house in Woburn Sands which is a fairly large village just outside Milton Keynes. It was a brand new semi-detached house and had a very small garden, three small bedrooms, sitting room, kitchen and a garage to the side. I landscaped the garden with a path using marble from the shopping centre that the contractors had given to me, a small lawn and some shrubs. The garden backed onto an industrial site with a mature hedge so it was quite private. Again, I returned to being quite lonely socially and hadn't made any friends. I went over to Bedford to get a haircut and liked the place. Eventually, I found a girlfriend there and we became close. We were in fact, together for fourteen years. I used to visit my mam every few weeks because she was still on her own, as she would be for the rest of her life. I would help her with the garden and especially when she moved houses which she did on a couple of occasions. By this time my sister and her husband had started their life in Kathmandu, Nepal. Her husband employed in development work for UNICEF which was very active in that area in health and nutrition because the country was very poor. He devoted his life to this work and what better start than Nepal with its wonderful scenery and people?

My relationship with my girlfriend although quite close, was not what one could describe as stable. I did love her but she was quite insecure because of other failed relationships and she also had health problems, heavy and severe migraines which she still suffers from. I was able to help her in some ways and we had some nice holidays and breaks away together. Because of the fragile relationship I needed some independence and had several holidays on my own. One was to Athens in Greece and Santarini. We had quite a good social life, going to numerous night clubs. Whilst I did not have a business, I also did not have a relationship that I could totally commit myself to. I decided to that it would be a good idea to take at least one more trip to Nepal while I still had independence. I went to visit my sister and her family. They had settled down well and he was enjoying his job. They also now had two young girls. My sister, her husband and other friends had gone for walks in Scotland with me and I loved these days up in the clouds. It was a natural attraction for me to go trekking and sample the Nepalese culture. I set off with heightened anticipation and I was not disappointed. I had a three week holiday there and what a treat and an adventure it was. I was treated so nicely, not only by my sister and her husband, but also by their two servants and the guide and the porter that I went trekking with. The lady servant did the cooking and the housework while her husband tended the grounds. They lived at the bottom of the garden in a small house and I guess they had some children. Before I went on my own trekking, I went with Michael (my sister's husband) on a short trek with a lovely Nepalese colleague of his called Navesh. It was a short trek, not strenuous but a lot of fun and Michael had a wicked sense of humour. We were away for perhaps three or four days and it was a good taster of things to come. The Nepalese colleague was a lovely soft man and I guess he was a Ghurka with his determination and humility, common to the Nepalese people. We walked through the most beautiful countryside and it was a good way to get fit for a longer or more strenuous trek. I had done some walking at home prior to going there to get myself fit.

One trek I will always remember, in one place we had to climb a cliff step by step as you would with stairs and we also had the anticipation of the excellent views when we reached the top as it was always different and stunning. I do not like heights so I tried not to look down and just bit the bullet. I always remember one particular bed and breakfast that we stayed in, we slept in the roof with the chickens! We were woken up early and had to avoid their droppings! All of this was a very special experience for me and a long way from Milton Keynes, as Michael joked. It all whetted my appetite for a trek I was yet to embark on, on my own with just a guide and porter. The socializing and humour added an extra dimension to the experience, especially when you came to rest under a Ficus tree (as in Ficus Benjamina, the well- known house plant) and have a glass of chia, a black sweet tea served in a glass. This was good to keep hydrated and to supply some energy. The Ficus trees were considered holy and were never cut down. One thing that did shock me was the poor hygiene standards, I guess akin to pre- Victorian times here in the UK. You could even call it medieval. People would defecate almost anywhere and so the cafes were swarming with flies. I especially remember one occasion, a little child defecated directly down a steep cliff without any fear at all!

After this shorter trip I decided to organise a longer one for myself to Annapurna Base Camp. I hired a guide and porter and off we went. Again, a lovely experience going through the villages, starting with paddy fields, ridges and valleys with lots of vegetation. These included trees and shrubs that we use as garden plants such as cherries and rhododendrons etc. The porter did most of the hard work, carrying most of my luggage plus the camping equipment because it was our plan to camp out in the Annapurna sanctuary. All of this he did without complaint. We even took along cooking utensils as we planned to have a meal up there out in the open. On the way we got a lovely view of Machapuchare, never climbed as it was very steep and was also considered to be very holy as are most mountains. On the way through the last village we decided to purchase a live chicken for our special meal. On this trip I also recall that I had a bottle of the local brandy, Actually, it is not really brandy, but industrial alcohol flavoured with caramel but imbibed as a drink. It keeps you warm and is an excellent night cap. As we approached the sanctuary, the guide suggested that we kill the chicken out of respect for the Gods in the mountains. It was pretty cold in the sanctuary and there was a covering of snow but, after erecting the tents, we had a nice meal and probably a few brandies for me. In the morning, when we awoke, there was a beautiful sunrise over the Annapurna range of perhaps five peaks which cast a magnificent shadow over the sanctuary. A sight to behold and I took several photos with my simple Olympus Trip. After that it was time to pack and head back to Rokene and then on to Kathmandu.

A few years later, I went with an older work colleague, who was a bit of a hippy with his beard and long hair, so he jumped at the opportunity. He was quite nervous about the whole thing

I believe he had never travelled much before. We went to Bangladesh, Dacca and then on to Kathmandu because it was the cheapest airline. We arrived in Dacca sometime during the day and it was supposed to be an hour's stop over before travelling on to Kathmandu. A few hours went by and nothing seemed to be happening and I went to politely ask what was going on. They informed me that they had a mechanical problem; in fact, they had only four Boeing 707's and they were all on the tarmac. They said that they were trying to get one fixed. Later, we were told that our connecting flight wouldn't be leaving that evening and they would put us up in a local hotel and we had to hand over our passports before leaving the airport. What an experience that turned out to be! Dirty is a polite way to describe the hotel room. If you touched the bedside lamp, a cloud of dust rose into the air. We risked eating a meal of curry but were warned against drinking the local water. I was quite happy to survive on gin and tonic. In the morning we looked around the local markets before going back to the airport. The first thing we did was collect our passports, not quite so easy for me and this is where the surprise came about. An immigration officer or maybe an employee of the airline told me that I could only have my passport if I purchased a bottle of whisky. What choice did I have?! It certainly caused me to panic a bit. I consulted with Brian and we agreed that I had no choice but to go and buy the booze. We went through immigration and nobody came forward, it was only when were on the tarmac and about to board the plane, that the officer brought me my passport to exchange for the bottle of whisky. This was obviously common practice because he did all of this in full view of his colleagues despite it being a Muslim country. As for me, I just let out a long sigh of relief!

When we arrived in Kathmandu we stayed with my sister and her family once again. After a day or two around Kathmandu valley we made our plans to go out trekking. I had to be careful because Brian was quite a bit older than me and not very fit. I felt responsible for him but, in fact, he did very well. Soon, we were ready to set off for Muckinath, a town in quite a high and remote area to the East of Kathmandu. It seems that each time I visited Nepal it was different but always the same stunning landscapes. We climbed higher and the vegetation all but disappeared and it became very much like a moonscape. Up there, the precipitation was minimal and it can be really cold for most of the year. What the people survive on I have no idea but I assume it would have been handicrafts because the farms were subsistence only. I remember when we arrived at the last village, we must have been at an altitude of around 10,000 feet because the air was so thin. The roofs of the houses were virtually flat so that any rainwater would not be wasted. The locals also appeared to have a much darker skin tone compared to the usual golden brown complexion of the Nepalese. After asking our guide about this, he told us that these people never bathe from the day they are born, newborns are just rubbed with oil. If they were to use water to bathe a newborn it would cause a cold or pneumonia and the loss of the infant. Back then we went to Pokhara, admiring the landscape as we went with its beautiful waterfalls. One unexpected surprise was when we came across some hot springs where we communally bathed and cleaned ourselves up. One thing that did amuse us was that Brian had a fascination for butterflies which were plentiful at the lower levels. When our guide or porter saw one, they would shout, "Pudali!" which is the Nepalese word for Butterfly. Brian would then rush over to get a photo. They nicknamed him 'Jessopa' which means 'old man with a beard'. Although I had gone to Milton Keynes to further my career and to start a business, all of these experiences were an additional bonus and something I could never have dreamt of. After that trip to the mountains we went down to what is called The Terai in Nepal. It was a fairly flat area and was also the most productive are agriculturally. It also had a nature reserve where you could view Rhinos and Tigers but, I think even back then, the tigers were almost extinct. The viewing is done from the back of an Elephant and was all rather exciting!

When we returned home, we presented a slide show for friends and colleagues in a local pub and this turned out to be a very entertaining evening. Moving forward I decided it would be best for me to approach a contractor to do sub-contract work for him but he declined. I later heard that he declined because he thought I was not serious. How wrong he was! Perhaps a year or two later, I approached another contractor who accepted my proposal. He already used a retired colleague to help him with his business. I could not start work on my own for another two years as it was considered that I would have an unfair advantage knowing the process etc, I think rather unfounded. In the end, and with hindsight, this proved to be quite a bonus. I learned a lot and was able to produce a business plan after going on a business course and doing my own research. Of course, I had to choose someone to sub-contract to who I respected and trusted. I made plans to leave the corporation and Charlie, the contractor, was able to help me to find a truck from one of his contacts.

At weekends I used to go and do work in private gardens and sometimes I needed help with this. I was busy seven days a week but that was fine because I was single. I was enjoying the fresh air, the freedom and the healthy lifestyle. I never liked any office job and being beholden to someone else and I loved this new challenge. As with my last departure, I organised a leaving party and again, it went over the top! Colleagues and contractors were invited to a nice local pub where we occupied the whole of the upstairs bar, there must have been more than fifty people there. I bought the first round of drinks as people arrived. They brought me lots of presents and a 'grannygram', I sat on her lap as she read a dirty story to me which I still have to this day. The cards were nice because two of the architects were very good at drawing cartoons. Charlie and I decided that we wouldn't say where I was going to work, we didn't want it to spoil the party by becoming the main topic of conversation. After that, we had a few more drinks back at the office and I believe I attended another party after all that and so had a very late night. The next morning, Saturday, I was able to get up early in the morning and go to Kidlington to do some work on a private garden. The two years were up and it was time to start my plan to set up my own business. I'm sure that Charlie knew about my plans but this was all good experience and hardened me up to the commercial world.

As time went on, I attended a free, sponsored Government business course at the weekends over in Buckinghamshire which I found to be very useful and it boosted my confidence. I learned as much, if not more from my fellow students as I did from the lecturer who was a failed businessman. Most of the students already had their own businesses and were able to speak from experience and tell me all the 'do's' and 'don'ts'. We worked on cash flows and the business which gave me a solid start. You had to do this in contracts as often you would not be paid on time and had to have a fall back plan. I was amazed and somewhat annoyed when I approached the National Westminster bank to arrange overdraft facilities. I went to them because I had been with them since I was sixteen and was now approaching thirty four or five. I met the manager and presented him with my business plan. His response was to lean back in his chair and laugh at me saying that there were already enough gardeners in the area as far as he could see. I was rather taken aback but I kept my cool and had a little think about what to do next. I asked him if it was true that a local garden and landscape firm had an account with him and that they were millionaires, he agreed. I then said, 'Well, if I can have a few crumbs from their table then that will be enough for me!' He then became a little more serious and accepted my business plan and arranged an overdraft facility. I started my business in the early Spring which was the busiest time and I was able to get work easily and never needed to use the overdraft facility. Gradually, I was able to buy equipment like a tractor and a lorry from my profits. A few years later, I DID get some work from the millionaire gardening firm, more on that later...

My social life in Milton Keynes was almost non-existent, however, I was well occupied with the business. I was still seeing the same girlfriend and occasionally going to nightclubs and pubs.
****
* The pub culture enabled me to do most of my recruiting and I think that I started off with just one or two young guys with a few other men to help out at the weekends. My business got off to a good start, I was working six and a half days each week and doing my paperwork in the evenings and in any other spare time that I had. Even in those early days I was having to turn work away and I didn't want to take too much on. I had seen other contractors take on too much and be unable to maintain their standards. Working for MKDC meant that payments were made promptly after about a month or even less. Due to this I had a healthy cash flow and was able to but equipment and expand my business. Within perhaps three months, I was able to buy a second-hand Massey Ferguson 135 which was ideal for my business. It also had a rotovator and grader and was ideal for grass seeding wide. This tractor lasted me for the twenty three years that I ran my business and never gave me any trouble.

As well as working during the week for the Development Corporation, I was able to work weekends on private gardens due to various contacts, notably building and landscape architects. Later on, I was able to sub-contract to a roadworks contractor doing mainly grass seeding. I then started working for house building contractors, mainly doing tidying and planting front gardens and public areas. These were all people who I had become acquainted with during my MKDC days. In hindsight, it's not always what you know but who you know. I had a range of suppliers for various materials such as fertilizers, seeds, bulbs, plants, composts and mulches, all gained from my time at MKDC. Things were beginning to fall into place quite nicely. Many evenings were spent doing paperwork, doing the pricing, filling in the tenders, day to day accounts, VAT and wages. This meant that I had a very full life with very little time for socialising except for with my girlfriend who liked to go to nightclubs. I managed to rent some space in a farmyard where Brian also operated from. In fact, I never paid any rent and just trimmed the hedges in the farmer's extensive garden once a year. Not long after, I decided to buy a three and a half ton Beffen flatbed lorry from the same guy who supplied my truck. This made life a lot easier because I could load the rotovator onto it for jobs that were out of town and it would also carry large amounts of plants. Compost, mulches and soil could also be carried to various sites on the flatbed which in turn, enabled me to expand my business quite rapidly. The only thing missing from my life was a truly trusting and loving relationship and someone to just simply share my life with.

I had a stroke of luck that enabled me to expand my business further and become more independent. A local businessman and farmer had decided to divide a large field into paddocks which he had grass seeded and fenced, each had an independent source of water and electricity available. These were then put up for sale at a local auction in the village hall. The paddocks were only about two miles from my house at that time. I surveyed the plots and declined the first one because it was triangular in shape and also beside a public footpath. The other three were, in my opinion, ok. I thought I might start off bidding for the second one and took my cheque book with me just in case. I sat with a few friends including the farmer who was selling the land and another local farmer. The first plot went for an acceptable price. When the second one came up, a bid was out on and I discreetly put up my finger to add £500. After my bid there was, surprisingly, no other bid. I had an eight acre paddock and had only paid £22,500 for it. The other tow plots were then sold, the last one for a ridiculously high price. The man must have been desperate to get it and he was given a rather sarcastic round of applause when the bidding was over. After the auction, the farmer that I had been sitting next to asked me who had bought the second plot which surprised me somewhat. Upon finding out that it was me, he was shocked and said that he had not seen me make my bid. When I enquired further, I found out that the other people there thought that the farmer had made the bid himself. Being a rich man, nobody would compete with him and so any competition would melt away. It taught me the importance of luck, being discreet and sitting next to someone who is known to be loaded!

I now had more than enough to keep me busy, to make my business more flexible and to further expand. When not so busy, we could work on the paddock and not fight for work. It came to my notice that MKDC were selling a disused barn by closed tenders, I put in a bid and was successful. It was some twenty metres by thirty metres, of metal construction with an asbestos roof and cladding for about one or two metres from the roof. I had to arrange for a local contractor to dismantle it and re-erect it in the paddock which will be known, going forward, as the depot. Before it was re-built, the metal was brushed and given a couple of coats of rust resistant paint. It cost me more to do all of this than it had cost me to buy the barn in the first place but it was all well worth it. Everything went well and I began to construct a breeze block wall with an outer skin of cheap bricks. I got some of the breeze blocks free from building sites because they were leftovers. I only had to use my labour and my lorry to transport the bricks to the depot. This work was done in the summer months when it was not so busy. At the same time, we built storage and car parking out of road tarmac shavings. I also had a storage area for pot plants where I could keep them watered. I decided that the best location for the barn would be in the lowest corner next to the service road, then it wouldn't impose on the site. Perhaps, in the short term, this was not the best location because that summer there was heavy rain. All the run-off found its way onto the barn floor which had not, fortunately, been concreted. I had some grass seed in there on pallets and the water reached the top of these pallets, fortunately the seed was not damaged.

I also constructed a small pond with an island, making use of the JCB which was already on site. The topsoil I used to increase soil depths in the areas I was yet to plant for windbreaks, the subsoil I used to create bands and increase security. Prior to digging, I asked a soil surveyor to visit and he advised me not to excavate too deep as there was a seam of sand about two and a half metres down. If this was breached, the pond would lose water, we were diligent in this matter. I had a roller door fitted to the barn for the main entrance and, when it was in place, I warned the JCB driver but he still managed to dent it on day one! I contacted a local metal contractor (who had made ramps for the lorry) and asked him to make some windows and a security door. The windows were plastic coated and double glazed in plastic as well for added security. Next, I had electricity run in from the transformer that was on my plot. So now I had electricity for lighting and security. BT installed a phone line meaning that the alarm could be linked up to the phone to deter intruders. I was warned of any attempt at trespassing because I had beams put across the car park and storage areas and alarms fitted to the barn. A fob was needed to disable it upon entry.

In the Autumn and Winter, I decided to plant Alder whips to grow up a windbreak on two sides of the depot, hedges bordered the other two boundaries. The whips were attached to wires using old inner tubes. Later on, every single one of the Alders was removed and sold to one of the workers. Later, I ploughed and rotovated a three metre wide strip on three sides to grow various trees and shrubs. When we had some time on a Saturday, we would go to the local stables to get some manure and spread it around the trees as a mulch. As time went by, my business continued to expand and I was making a reasonable profit every year. At the end of each financial year when I knew my rough profit and what I had in the bank I would pay lump sums into a number of private pensions. This also had the advantage of reducing my tax bill. I also decided that I could afford to move to a better house as the present one had little potential for improvement. I found a house in Woburn, about a five minute drive from the depot.

It was a traditional red brick house, about fifteen years old at that time and was located at the end of a gravel cul-de-sac. I was quite stunned by the then present owners, he, being a mortgage broker at Natwest bank, the place was falling apart so he must have been very busy at work! Some of the wallpaper was falling off, the carpets dirty and worn, window frames and doors rotting and far from secure and the kitchen units were falling apart. The bathroom was an out of date avocado colour. I felt sorry for the house but at least I would be able to fit it out to my taste. Perhaps this was a once in a lifetime opportunity as I was never one for moving around much.

Starting at the beginning, I had to choose my priorities carefully but I was happy with the challenge. The garden to the rear, although quite small, about fifteen metres by seven, had potential. It was secluded with fencing and a Leyland hedge and the soil was good sandy loam. The first thing I had done was the windows and doors replacing with white plastic double glazed ones. This made it secure and much cosier and easier to maintain. The contractors were very diligent and did a perfect job on them. I then went to Bedford for the bathroom and cloakroom suites and a local plumber/fitter was recommended to me. However, he wasn't so good and I knew whenever he'd been because there would be cigarette butts outside the back door which he had thrown out of the window. He was slap-dash and careless and, what really annoyed me, he allowed tile offcuts to fall into the bath and damage and fracture the surface. I had made a mistake and kept back no reserve so, when I found the damage it was too late and I couldn't get him to come back. Lesson learnt!

The next project was the kitchen which again I chose from a local showroom, this time in Milton Keynes and they also carried out the fitting. I chose locally manufactured materials because it would be easier to replace if necessary. The fitters were not as bad as the plumber but not so good either. After some heated discussions, work got underway and was mostly done to my satisfaction, looked good and functioned well. The main mistake they made, which I hadn't noticed was that they had installed the gas hob next to the fridge freezer so that the flames damaged the surface. Later on, I got some grey asbestos sheet to protect the surface. After all this, I got the house redecorated, carpeted and curtains hung, the predominant colour being light blue and grey. Now it felt like home!

Finally, I was able to pay some attention to the garden. The front was largely brick paved so did not need much attention. There I grew a specimen tree plus some climbers and shrubs by the kitchen window. Originally, I planted a Cordyline specimen but that succumbed to frosts. I replaced it with a large pine from the depot. I had a lot of fun with the back and took my time over it. Later in life, after I married and had a family, it became a nice place to sit and relax after a hard day's work. It faced East and was in the shadow of the house except for the bottom part that caught the evening sun. Here is where I installed a sunken patio area and a pergola and trellis to make the garden more private. The pergola I painted with black stain and the trellis I painted red and planted with a clematis in blue of course, my favourite colour. I used York stone for the dwarf wall and rockery because it is longer lasting and best around water, I planned to install two little adjoining ponds. The two ponds would be interconnected with two waterfalls operated by an electric pump. I was able to plant a prostrate conifer to droop over the waterfall. I put goldfish in the ponds with waterlilies and aerating weeds.

It had a yellow theme with the odd flash of red. I re-laid a small area of lawn and the garden was very easy to maintain. So it was, I did all the hard work, created a nice environment to live in and was making a reasonable profit with my business. But I was a lonely man. One day I found that I had over £22,500 in my pocket and gave it to my girlfriend to enable her to buy her council house which she still has today. I also bought her a yellow, second-hand Fiesta car and taught her to drive. Later on, someone put sugar in the petrol tank and the same person, or maybe someone else, put acid all over the roof. Whether this was jealousy or racially motivated I will never know. She is a black Jamaican lady who I am still friends with now.

The pond at the depot I also planted with waterlilies and aerating weeds. I added a few Perch, they multiplied at an alarming speed and made a good meal for the local Heron! I built a bridge to the island that could be drawn up at night so the ducks would be safe during the hours of darkness. However, there was something potentially missing from my life that I have previously alluded to. I hadn't yet found the person that I could truly trust and live with. Someone who I could spend my life with and share the benefits of my labours. I distinctly remember one evening, sitting on the patio steps with a glass of wine in one hand and a cigarette in the other, gazing up at the blue sky. I prayed to God to send that friend to me. A couple of years later, my prayers were answered from an unexpected quarter. Until then, I still had to suffer quite a lot of pain, but that's where you get the gain, so they say. I still had little in the way of a social life other than with my girlfriend and the odd trip to the local pub. It was unlikely that I would meet anyone. Every Friday I would spoil myself with a Chinese takeaway and a bottle of Moet champagne, all the while craving for that special someone.

Over quite a long period, I found that running the business was a lonely affair because I chose not to have a business partner. Every evening I would do all the paperwork accompanied by a glass of wine, or three! The loneliness caused me to develop anxiety and I was worrying unnecessarily about the business. I took on tasks that I was not profiting from like constructing steps and walls and not trusting any of my workers to undertake them. This was a misplaced lack of trust and I need not have worried at all. As with most worrying, it was a waste of time and without any foundation. However, my anxiety increased as I took on more work and employed more labour. After some time, I knew that I had become clinically depressed. Sleep was sporadic, I didn't want to get up in the morning and I had a lot of trouble making simple decisions. I couldn't even decide which toothbrush to use! It was difficult for me to motivate myself, even to go and get my hair cut. In the end, I went to see my doctor. He agreed with my diagnosis but did not enquire about my drinking which was getting progressively worse. The doctor gave me a choice of two treatments; antidepressants or counselling. I opted for the tablets as a quick fix and, in some ways, they did work.

DIFFICULT TIMES AND A MIRACLE

At my lowest point, when perhaps I had reached rock bottom, I received a call from my mum. She had a letter from Marta, after all that time! It was probably some twenty two years since I had seen her (hence the title of this book!) Unusually, my mum had opened the letter which is something that she had never done before. God was on my side and my prayers had been answered. In the letter, Marta explained that she was coming to Bath for three weeks to do an English course again and gave me a contact number for her intended lodgings. Three or four days later, when I guessed that she'd be in, I rang her from a phone box on my way home from seeing a client in Luton. I didn't have a mobile phone in those days and I could not wait until I got home to call her. I guess I was excited to meet someone again who I had liked so very much. It seemed very strange to talk to her again after such a long time and under such strange circumstances. Anyway, we went through the usual formalities because we could hardly discuss other matters over the phone. We agreed to meet on the following Saturday in Bath. Marta said she had a plan for when we met so I had some sort of an idea what might happen when we did meet again and looked forward to it with much anticipation! We arranged to meet outside the Abbey at twelve noon and agreed that we would recognize each other; this is how it proved to be. I left the depot after leaving some work for my employees and, dressed smartly but informally, set off in my little Honda car.

As I waited in the square, I finally saw her and was struck by her longer hair but, more importantly, at around twenty metres away, she began to appear rather sad. When I approached her, I gave her a gentle kiss on the cheek and said hello before remarking, 'Is that still the same perfume that you wore years ago?!' To which, she replied, 'Yes.' That was so unlike me but it was a rather lingering perfume, Miss Dior, which I still buy for her now on special occasions. From there we agreed to go on a short trip on the river and then on the open topped bus for a tour of the city. Following this she asked to go to Bristol which I reluctantly agreed to, I would have preferred to stay in Bath. I don't remember seeing anything special except for the waterfront from a distance. We visited a number of churches and she told me about her life in Slovakia. She explained that she was married with three young daughters. She told me about their education and the hardships under Communist rule. She spoke nothing of her husband which I found rather strange but I didn't enquire further. We stopped for a drink at a pub and I was amused that the man behind the bar had such a strong accent that I couldn't understand him and let him keep the change! We agreed, upon returning to Bath, that it would be nice to have a meal together. After looking around for what felt like ages, we ended up at the Hilton Hotel which appeared ok and had a pianist in the restaurant. I was amazed when Marta's meal arrived, it was fish in a paper bag! It looked very unappetising. I asked her if she particularly wanted it and we decided it wasn't good enough. We left without eating.

By this time is was approaching 10pm and we found a pub called The White Bear and had some drinks and crisps. The conversation must have gone a little quite as Marta is a lady of few words. I knew that I still loved her but I didn't know how she felt about me. We must have only been there for a matter of fifteen minutes when I suddenly blurted out, 'Marta, I think we should be married.' It certainly wasn't my plan to say it, it just came out of my mouth! She looked at me, not overly shocked, and just said that she would have to think about it. Well, fair enough! When you are in love, you don't think of rejection. Later, she agreed for me to stay at her lodgings so I didn't have to travel home that night. When we got to her place, we asked permission from her landlady who replied, 'Be careful of that man, there's a full moon tonight.' Marta was not keen to be intimate but, I guess you might say, I wouldn't take no for an answer and she reluctantly agreed. The following day is a bit hazy, well, it is a few years ago now! I do remember that she said she wanted to buy a dress and we found ourselves in BHS. She took a long time to decide on a dress, nowadays I know it's just her way. She finally chose one and reluctantly, allowed me to pay for it. We also did a lot of walking and visited The Crescent housing area at the top of Bath where there was a nice view over the city. We had some lunch and, in the evening, went to a Heritage Hotel and had a lovely meal that somewhat made up for the previous evening. I have since learned that she loves fish and that night we both had the Dover Sole, delicious. It was made all the more romantic because there was a pianist playing in an adjacent room. The following day, Saturday, it was time to say goodbye and I escorted her back to her lodgings. We had agreed that she would come to visit me in Woburn on the following weekend and the weekend after that she was due to go back to Bratislava. In the event, on the weekend she was due to visit me, she caught the bus to Aylesbury and I picked her up from there.

We spent two days together again and once again I didn't ask her questions about her husband or any plans for the future. For perhaps the first time in my life, I was patient. I cannot remember if I cooked for her, not being very talented in that department but I must have cooked us some breakfast. We must have gone for a Chinese meal since that's her favourite. I do remember her walking around the house and garden, weighing it all up to see if it met the needs of her and her daughters. This did not please me because I realised that if they were going to come and live with me, it would mean a huge sacrifice due to their close family ties. At some stage over the weekend we went up to Milton Keynes city centre where we visited the Water Gardens which had been designed by a landscape architect friend of mine and installed by Frosts who I later worked for. It was a lovely environment with the indoor plants at different levels, Cotswold walls, a pool and waterfalls. I have p a lovely photo of her taken there.

The next weekend she was going back to Bratislava and I believe I went down to Bath to take her and we stayed near Heathrow airport because she had an early morning flight to catch. As before, we found it difficult to find a place to eat and once again, we ate crisps and had some drinks but, this time, we had champagne. We enjoyed each other's company and spent a lovely night together, she seemed more relaxed now. When I took her to the airport the next morning, she said she would write to me and we agreed that we needed to be discreet with regard to our relationship so as not to upset her family. I think we also agreed for me to go and visit Bratislava to further explore our relationship. I seem to remember that she was not long in writing to me, perhaps a week. Amazingly, I did not fret as I normally might because our relationship was already based on love and trust. I do remember telling friends that I had met the love of my life again. When she had written to me, she had expressed her love for me with the words from a Bryan Adam's song, 'Everything I do, I do it for you'. I did not know the song or the words so I rang my niece in Scotland to ask her where it came from. After it was explained to me, I bought the tape and returned the sentiment, again using a Bryan Adam's song 'Please Forgive Me' which described so aptly, my love for her and in a much better way than I could ever do. From then on, I fund it quite hard to concentrate on my work. I am lucky enough to have my memories reinforced by the letters that I wrote to her, I am able to re-read them and they are so precious to me. They remind me of the understanding we had, and still have, for each other. Later, under trying circumstances, she had quietly given them back to me and I still have them to this day. I'm a little shocked at some of the things I wrote because they were quite passionate but they alleviated some of the frustration at not being with her. I was expressing my love for her, my feelings and memories as a way of encouraging her because it was not easy for her being in the matrimonial home. This is why I sometimes say, beware what you throw away and that includes relationships.

Around a month or so later, I took my first trip to Bratislava via Vienna as that was the easiest way to get there at the time. A friend of hers, Peter, came to the airport with her and took me into Bratislava. He arrived in a fairly old Skoda which gave him a bit of trouble on the journey. He got quite messy trying to remedy the engine problem but he made not a word of complaint. As time went by, he also became a good friend of mine. It was nice to see Marta again and see some of her family, particularly her three girls and her parents. She had asked me to stay at a hotel halfway between her work and her home. She later described the hotel as being frequented by ladies of ill repute, money launderers and I guess, also, drugs. She worked at a bank as an English teacher to help the staff when they went abroad on business. She also did evening classes at a private language school as well as giving some private tuition. With her family commitments too, she was kept busy but without a word of complaint.

The room in the hotel was comfortable and about six floors up so I had a reasonable view of the city and it was easy for Marta to visit me and she did so most days, sometimes twice. Even back then there were some lovely restaurants so we either had a drink or went out for a meal. Most of the places were really smart and the waiters were friendly and helpful. Remember, this was a country not long to have cast off the shackles of Communism and, as I later learned, not all bad, as was life in general. German is the preferred second language to serve the German and Austrian tourists who, like me, found the prices amazingly cheap. They also enjoyed the numerous spas, skiing and walking. Bratislavian people do not often visit Slovakia, preferring the Czech republic. I had to spend quite a lot of time on my own, so most days I would go walking to familiarise myself with the city often getting lost and quite tired.

Marta was as attentive as she could be under the circumstances, she made a special effort to meet up with me as much as possible and took me to meet some of her family. The way that she arranged things was very clever and considerate. I am not sure how much we achieved on my first visit but I went home well satisfied, it had been a lovely experience of icebreaking. I had a meal with an old friend of Marta's called Duscan, who was a lawyer of good repute and he was a very capable man. They had been close friends for quite a while, having met some years ago at a nearby spa. He had been there because of his disabilities a firework had hit him on the top of his head during a display. They helped me to choose my meal and it was delicious. This was also the restaurant that Marta chose for me to meet her two eldest daughters. She did something quite amazing for this although I'm not sure that the girls liked it much. She dressed them in lovely light blue dresses and they looked like twins although there's at least a year between them. They were naturally quiet, especially the younger girl. But who could blame them? Meting a strange man from England who was to become a large part of their young lives. Whether they realised it or not I don't know because I had hardly grasped the enormity of what I was doing myself. The younger girl nodded and agreed with everything her sister said and there was a nice atmosphere considering it was our first meeting and I was a complete stranger to them. To put them at their ease, I asked them who their favourite band was. One replied that it was Guns 'n' Roses and the younger sister nodded in agreement. After the meal we went a short distance, I took a photo of them standing in front of a light blue Catholic church and of course, it matched their dresses. I had yet to meet the third, and youngest daughter, who was only five years old. Again, Marta put a lot of thought into it as she knew that first impressions would mean a lot. She arranged that we met at a bus stop and we would go a little way out of town to a lovely natural park where we could all have a walk together. Initially, I was introduced as a friend, nobody special. The three of us walked through the park on a lovely summer's day, past ponds and streams. It was all very pleasant and the girl seemed to take to me as I ran about with her being quite playful. There just seemed to be a positive chemistry and I tried to be as natural as possible. There could be no verbal communication because she didn't speak any English but she just skipped happily along in the warm summer air. I can't be sure but I think we had an ice cream or a snack.

I pondered what the future would hold, lots of challenges no doubt. We would be strangers living under the same roof and I, an older man, rather set in his ways. I also realised that I was going to be responsible for their education and general wellbeing. Girls would be a challenge and Marta would have to get used to living in a strange country with different customs. She would also need to eventually find a job because she would not be happy being a housewife. With hindsight, we were taking a huge risk, it could all have led to heartache for all concerned but, for some reason, I had no fear. I only wanted the best for them. I have always been up for a challenge but this was to be the biggest one of my life so far. After I had been in Bratislava a few days, Marta bought a single rose to my hotel room from her neglected garden. As I found out later, the house was like a building site and her husband had no interest in flowers or gardens except for maybe vegetables. I was amazed to see the single rose and, of course, Marta didn't know the name of it. She and our daughters, as I can now call them, have come to mean so much to me as my continuing story will relate. They have, in so many ways, made me the man I am today. Back to the rose... Marta didn't know its name but, having a horticultural background, I knew straight away the name of this particular type because they grew in a rose bed at Lillyputts. It was a bloom with rich green leaves, a yellow flower with a pink flush and a sweet scent, of course it went by the lovely name of 'Peace'. To me, this rose was a gift of love from God.

I had always planned to formally propose to her and thought

this was an appropriate time. I was in no doubt that it was the right decision for both of us and it would be good for me to confirm my commitment to her. It was good that we had similar values and it was easy for us to sort out priorities. Her giving me hat Peace rose, although a simple act, had made me very happy. I bought some red roses and a bottle of chilled champagne. After she had been in the room for a little while I got down on one knee, presented her with the roses and proposed marriage to her. She accepted it with a smile, we embraced and sealed it with a kiss.

On another occasion, she took me out of town, in the family Skoda estate car, to a lovely restaurant where we were able to enjoy a typical Slovakian meal that you might eat at Christmas. It was a goose with potato pancakes and sweet and sour red cabbage made with natural vinegar and sugar. Of course, we enjoyed the meal with a glass of wine. There was a gypsy group playing which created a nice atmosphere. These are all wonderful memories that will never leave me. Now, as I write down my memories, I remember Marta's special friend, Duscan.

He was a family friend of some years who was very special. He would do all sorts of favours, not accepting any praise although he had his own two daughters to look after. When I was on my visit, as he did on many other visits, he would cook us a meal with some wine or champagne. I have to mention, the Slovakians call it champanski and it is also available in rose and red. At that time, it was only one pound a bottle! They would start by including me in their conversation but Duscan's spoken English was not good and they would drift into Slovakian. Being a bit selfish back then, I would get rather resentful, drink a bit too much and then fall asleep. Duscan allowed me to keep in regular contact with Marta when I was back in the UK. He worked for the National Telephone Company and would connect us in the evenings to have a free call which we did quite regularly. He nearly lost his job through this because Marta's husband got to know about it and reported him.

Now, as I write about my memories, I realise that I had a lot going on regarding my business and keeping in touch with Marta. I made regular visits to her and her girls and later, they started to visit me too. I knew there must have been quite a lot of friction between Marta and her husband and I think the eldest daughter got involved as well. I could easily make things a lot worse f I was not careful and had to be cautious about the decisions that I made. As I concentrated on these things, I rather neglected my business and my profit reduced by half, add to that the fact that it was a drought year.

I was lucky to have those letters and phone calls while I was in England and she was struggling back in Bratislava. In my letters I supported and encouraged her and spoke of our plans for the future with the girls being our main priority as well as Marta starting a new life. I think I also knew it would not be easy due to the prejudice against foreigners in the UK. I cannot remember the correct sequence of events because there was so much going on at the time.

Going back to my first visit and meeting her parents for the first time. Neither of them spoke any English so they spoke to me through Marta. Her mum said to me, through Marta, 'Please tell Clive, if he does not look after you and my granddaughters, I will kill him'. However, she said it with a smile and we never had a bad word between us. Another thing I remember is Marta coming to visit me in the New Year whilst telling her husband that she was on a language course at the Open University and I took a photo of her to prove it. She can be quite a scheming lady! Her husband was going through a hard time in his life and was falling apart. Who could blame him?

Not long after this we decided that she and the girls would move out of the family home to make life easier and more peaceful. Her family lived in a really big house of some twenty rooms and a large loft. It was near the city centre amongst the embassies, other large houses, bars and a pizzeria that we often used to frequent. The flat we rented was brand new, not far from her parents and a large market so it was ideal. Marta and her husband had renovated the house as it had been occupied by gypsies. She inferred that this was one of the reasons why their marriage was failing.

It was probably during the Easter holidays when Marta and the girls came to England for a week or so. Sometimes they would travel by bus, a very arduous trip of some thousand miles. This was less than a year since we had met again so things were moving along at a reasonable pace. Often, I would meet them at Heathrow airport if they had travelled by plane. As time went by, I would cook meals for them. They enjoyed eating English food but that doesn't take much skill to cook, they especially enjoyed it when I made spaghetti bolognese which I had introduced them to. Later on, Marta would make this when we were a family together. I also cooked anew recipe using prawns and celery which gave it a nice green colour. When we first got together, Marta would cook a really simple but colourful meal. Mashed potatoes, green spinach and a fried egg on top. It was a very healthy meal as well. We all seemed to get on well together and the girls were losing some of their shyness. I would visit Bratislava quite often and it was easier now because I could stay with them in the flat. It was an interesting and enjoyable experience.

It was on my second visit that I stayed in a different hotel. Her husband had become aware and visited the hotel whilst Marta was with me. There was a knock at the door which I answered and there stood her husband. He asked to speak with his wife, they had a short conversation and then he was gone. I asked what was said. He asked if we were in bed yet and she had replied, 'No, we're having a glass of wine and then going to bed after that'. She can be quite cheeky and naughty! Sometimes when I visited, we would go for trips outside of Bratislava and visit relatives. The family had a cottage in a large village. We would visit occasionally with her parents, stopping on the way back for mineral water. Her sister and family also used to come with us sometimes. Marta's sister's husband was a heavy snorer. On one occasion, he snored so much that the cottage shook. We also went to stay in a hotel which had a menu that what quite restricted. We went for lots of walks in the beautiful countryside and it was nice to relax and get to know one another.

On one occasion, I cannot remember the exact sequence, perhaps around eighteen months since I had met Marta again. It was around Christmas and New Year and we went to stay in a Slovak ski resort called Donnovaly. It was very cold and there was obviously plenty of snow around. I guess that we ate at local restaurants because we were staying in accommodation only, it wasn't a large resort. We visited the local Catholic church one Sunday and it was a nice experience although I didn't understand a single word of what was being said. However, there was a friendly and pleasant atmosphere. The two eldest girls were proficient skiers and, with the aid of the ski lifts, they were able to enjoy themselves. The young one did her best but it was too cold for her and she struggled to trudge to the ski lift with us, over half a kilometre away. Marta did all the driving at that time because I did not feel confident enough to drive over there. When we were loading up the car to come home Marta and I had our first tiff. As we were packing and strapping down the skis, she became frustrated and said that her husband would make a much better job of it. I thought that was a little unfair because I had never done this before and I tried to let it go and just do my best.

When they came to Woburn, we would go for walks over to the abbey and it was particularly beautiful when the rhododendrons were flowering. Our main priority was to find schools for the girls, they took their education very seriously as did their mother. Education in general is taken very seriously in Slovakia and I have always respected that. The eldest girl went to school in Vienna every day and the middle girl went to a school in Bratislava and the youngest across the border to Austria. She went every day in a little pink bus and when I was staying, I would go and pick her up to save her mum the trouble in her busy life. All three girls were also very good at languages. They were taught in German and had Slovak classes, one of them was also proficient in Russian. The little one gradually increased her knowledge of English with the help of her mum. Seeing how hard they had worked, I felt duty bound to find good schools for them. For the youngest one, it was quite easy because there was a very nice primary school in the next village and she was readily accepted there. It was a typical village primary with a caring headmistress so we knew she would be okay there. For the eldest two, it was not so easy and we visited quite a few state schools, some of which we found quite disappointing. There was one that we considered but it was a long bus ride away. When we visited Dame Alice school in Bedford, as it was known then, we quickly realised that it was place where the girls would progress. The headmistress engaged very positively with us and the girls and we were allowed to send them at a subsidised fee through The Harper Trust. It turned out to be a very good investment.

During this time, I was trying to run a business but obviously I was away quite a lot and busy with the family when they were visiting. In some respects, I came to realise 'When the cat's away the mice will play'. I knew that I had to be more careful because I now had a family to support. Added to this, I had to spend a lot of time going back and forth to immigration in Croydon to arrange the immigration papers. There was always plenty of queues and it also took me away from my work on a regular basis. It was like trying to juggle balls in the air but we slowly got there. Added to this, when Marta came by plane, I had to be there to see her through immigration and satisfy them that I could support her during her visit. It was all a bit humiliating but it had to be done.

To satisfy immigration, we had to organise a registry office wedding and the plan was to then have a church wedding in September when things had settled down. It was early June that we were first married, with my mum and two other friends as witnesses. One of the best aspects was that on the way back from the registry office in Amphill, we stopped for a few photos in Woburn park. The rhododendrons were in full bloom. After a meal together we spent the night in a pretty grotty pub and hotel. At that time, I was not good at finding the best places but it's much easier now with the internet.

Finally, about a month later, Marta and the girls packed up their most precious possessions, they could not bring too much because the house was quite small for five people and two of the bedrooms were very small indeed. They arrived in a small removal truck and were amongst the first people to utilise the Channel Tunnel. They travelled with Duscan and his wife which made things a lot easier for them. They arrived sometime in the afternoon and were extremely tired after a one thousand mile journey but still they found the energy to unpack. Marta insisted on doing the cooking on the first day, which, with hindsight, I should have done myself. As the seven of us sat down for our first meal as a family since we were married, Marta knocked over a glass of red wine. I thought nothing of this and went to the kitchen to fetch a cloth to wipe it up. There I found the oldest daughter crying and when I asked what was wrong, she replied, 'Do you not know that our mum is an alcoholic'? Harsh words that turned out to be true. This was quite a shock to me but I was not overly phased and only half realised the implications of the situation and how much of a problem it would become. It was to have quite a big influence as time went by. In some ways, at the beginning, I did not allow it to affect our relationship.

The girls settled in well at their schools but the middle daughter rather clung on to her older sister because she lacked confidence. Often, I think common in a child born prematurely as she was. But she also showed determination as did her sisters. They all encountered some prejudice, coming from a foreign country and having strange names. The headmistress and careers advisor were very supportive towards the girls. The young one got on well at her primary school due to the kindness of her headmistress. She also encountered prejudice for the same reasons as her elder sisters. This led to her later changing her surname to mine but the eldest two kept their father's name. Almost from the start, we began attending the Anglican church in nearby Woburn Sands. The one in Woburn was rather austere. Most of the congregation were very friendly, especially one lady who usually sat behind us. The youngest soon joined the choir and the two eldest were confirmed. I was rather disappointed with this as they were given very little instruction as I had been given when at school. In early September, Marta and I were married in this church. It was just a small ceremony with my sister and her husband on my side. Marta's sister and family came over. I appreciated their efforts to come over from Slovakia as this was the first time that any of them had been to the UK. Except for her father because he was a high up scientist in the aluminium industry. We had a choir and a few of the congregation attended which made it special for Marta and I. She looked beautiful in her pink wedding dress and matching hat and when we got home, I carried her across the threshold of the front door. We sat down to a special meal that Marta had prepared, no doubt with help from her mum. She was a very good cook or 'cooker' as our young daughter used to say. It was a proper family affair and we did a lot of dancing in the living room and outside in the garden. As the evening approached, Marta and I went to stay in a local hotel that she had booked and was made a lot nicer because we had the bridal suite. It was nice to get up in the morning and enjoy breakfast together in the conservatory that overlooked a patio and gardens. It was not long until we would go back home to the family, my sister and her husband having gone back to Scotland.

It was lovely to have Marta's family to stay and I don't know to this day how any of us managed to have a peaceful night's sleep as there were eleven of us. We were able to go for lots of nice walks around Woburn and Milton Keynes and also visit Cambridge and St. Albans. Cambridge became a favourite place of ours to visit as a family. On this occasion we went on an open topped bus for a tour of the city and it was a lovely day. I have many happy memories of our trip to Cambridge.

After our marriage in early September, straight after it was the start of the school term for the girls and back to work for me. The eldest two had to catch a bus to Bedford and Marta took the youngest to school by car because it was two or three miles away. I went to work each day and Marta kept herself busy as a home maker and a good mum which I came to respect because she had always done academic jobs. At the beginning she was not able to work, family and friends were far and wide and she does not make friends easily. Life was very tough for her.

MARRIAGE, WORK AND ROCK BOTTOM

As I have previously mentioned, I was on antidepressants when I met Marta again, partly due to loneliness but I was certainly not lonely now! I was feeling better within myself. So, with my GP's and Marta's permission, I gradually weaned myself off them. Life went on, Marta insisting that the girls had good lights in their bedrooms so they could study and me taking her out to practice her driving in different conditions. Not only did she learn to drive on the left side but also had to learn to negotiate all the roundabouts in Milton Keynes and not get lost. Getting lost was quite easy to do until she got use to things. She became a confident and proficient driver. But I think she still felt quite isolated, she had lost some of her family and friends back home, however, she did not complain. I didn't appreciate that back then as I do now.

At that time Marta had a habit of thinking that the grass was always greener on the other side. This would regularly manifest itself at mealtimes when she would complain about the education system, how poor the NHS was and how things were much better back home in Slovakia. I understood and, in some ways, it was true but there was nothing that any of us could do about it. I got rather frustrated, especially as mealtimes should be a time of reflection and peace to allow you to enjoy and digest your food. I did know that they had a good education system and that their hospitals were run with high standards of hygiene and better after care. For instance, they used to send patients to spas after they had had surgery. When you visit a hospital in Slovakia, you have to wear overshoes so you don't contaminate the floors with dirt from outside. She did have some good points in her opinions. All of this happened for me after a hard day's work and it also stifled any other conversation. With hindsight, I think it was her way of venting her feelings because she was feeing so lonely and had too much time to think. Being naïve, I thought our marriage would be a bed of roses and I tended to be a bit over sensitive and quickly became unhappy with the situation. Initially I would leave the table and go for a walk to clear my head. As time went on, I used alcohol to relieve the pain I was receiving. When they came to live with me, I was much happier than I'd been in long time. I was determined that they would still go home once a year. In that way they would be able to stay in touch with family and friends. It was mostly at Christmas, new Year and during school holidays that we would visit. Quite often, friends and relations of Marta's would come and visit us so we had a busy life.

It wasn't long before we bought a people carrier so that we could drive to Slovakia rather than travel by bus or plane. This enabled us to buy lots of local food and drink whilst in Bratislava. There were too many things to mention but we bought things like cold or fresh meats, cheese, cheap wine, beer, gin and champanski (cheap sparkling wine) white, pink and red and it only cost about £1 a bottle. We were saving money because everything was so much cheaper in Slovakia. As Marta's family had a cottage in the mountains, we would also visit there quite regularly. We went for lovely walks in the forest and wildflower meadows. Sheep were brought there for summer grazing and were milked to make a soft cheese called Bryndza which I didn't particularly like but the family did. They had blackcurrants and other fruits in the garden and a wood stove in the kitchen where her mum made blackcurrant jam and juice as well as did her general cooking. The fresh fruit was good for us!

As time went by, Marta would drink too much. One such occasion was at an office party in London, other social events and she would also drink alone. I came to know her as a binge drinker. She would fall asleep at various functions and I particularly remember that it happened at a church function in London. On occasion she would go to Slovakia on her own and come back to Heathrow and get of the plane drunk. I tried to be there for her but I didn't always find it easy. I got annoyed when she was verbally abusive towards me. At an office party in London, we became separated, she got drunk and I had to walk across the city to sober her up before we caught the train back home. On another occasion, at the wedding of our niece in Scotland, she went missing and was found drunk in the toilets by our other niece. She also got drunk at her sister's wedding in Bratislava. She started to dance and fell over backwards, banging and bruising her head. Her mother sat and shook her head. Throughout all of this, I was not so innocent either. I drove back to her drunk and I know I shouldn't have been driving. In this instance, I wasn't the most responsible either.

As a responsible father, I tried to be good to Marta and the girls and support and encourage them. I learned of the importance of their education through their mum. At time I would get a bit frustrated when Marta would make the youngest do her multiplication tables whilst we were out on walks in Woburn, trying to unwind and relax. Not very relaxing, especially when the child got the answer to a question wrong. She got there in the end thanks to her mum's persistence. Another duty I took seriously, was getting Marta used to living in England and getting her used to driving. I also began to teach the two eldest girls to drive. In Milton Keynes that's easy as there are plenty of quiet industrial estates. At the weekend they could practice parking and reversing etc. I started them off in a car park in Woburn and so it was that the girls passed their tests first time and became competent drivers.

After a couple of years, Marta became frustrated that she was unable to work and was not satisfied with being a home maker. She is a doctor in Psychology and was a competent English teacher for people with English as a second language (ESOL) She had been used to working in Bratislava as well as looking after her family. When we as a family made a trip to Disneyland, Paris, her work became a topic of conversation on the way back home. She decided, with support, to do voluntary work for the Citizens Advice Bureau in Bletchley. This eventually led her to work for several companies who offered skills training at local job centres to support people back into work. This was not easy work because a lot of the local clients weren't really interested in seeking worthwhile careers. Through this work she met two asylum seekers who became good family friends. One aspect of the work was that she got to travel to different offices on training courses and I was amazed at how lacking in confidence Marta still was. At weekends, I would have to drive with her to the venues because she feared getting lost. She now has a sat nav which is a huge help. She still lacks confidence in general. I guess she was never really independent with regard to travel as I was. The trip to Disneyland was a huge disappointment and not a patch on the original one in Los Angeles.

Over the years and months, I began to drink more. Initially, a variety of drinks as we were in Slovakia and there is a wide variety of drink available there from beer to plum brandy. Slovakians like to drink and are hospitable, friendly and humerous. They have quite a 'macho' culture centred around drinking but are rarely 'worse for wear' or causing trouble. I think that Europeans, in general, do not abuse drink as much as we in the UK do. But, when I was there, I was encouraged to drink. I loved the cold lager beers during the summer, the plum brandy in the winter and of course, the champagne and wine at any time! We were always taking a lot of drinks back home when we visited. I often drank more when visiting relatives and friends, I was bored because most of the conversation was in Slovak. So, I would drink and fall asleep. Back home as well, I would drink earlier and earlier in the day and, at about this time, I decided to stop drinking whisky. It would make me sick and give me the most terrible hangovers so I changed to drinking gin which never gave me any of these problems. In times gone by it was known as 'mother's ruin' and it nearly ruined me. I had always liked gin and tonic although I had experimented with most types of drink. The only ones that I never really touched were 'White Lightning' and 'Meths'. Eventually, I arrived at a point where I had to make a conscious decision not to drink before 11am.

I had to have a carpal tunnel operation on both of my hands and in stead of eight months off work, I only had four. As I started to recover, I redecorated the house from top to bottom with more sympathetic and warming colours, more suited to a family. I stripped off all the old paper and prepared the paintwork. Physically, it was quite testing but it was good to feel the strength coming back I to my hands. The girls were at school and Marta was at work so nobody knew what I was up to and how much I was drinking during the day. That was probably ten years before I had my final drink.

From that time on, things became progressively worse and I later learned that it is a progressive illness that I had. We would go on holiday to Slovakia, Turkey, Croatia and Thassos (a Greek island) and back to the UK to the Lake District, Scotland and to the seaside, to the places that I went to as a child. I did these things to keep the family happy and was using alcohol to self-medicate. By this point, I was taking gin to work with me. At the time, I was working on my own because the workload had dropped off and new work in Milton Keynes had reduced dramatically. The honeymoon was over. I was losing work due to being careless because of my drinking. I was lucky that it didn't end up with some sort of disaster, killing myself or someone else. As time passed by, as is common with drinking problems, I wanted to take my own life. I never did. I told myself it was a selfish act and I had also landed a large contract.

The client was very fussy and demanding but pleasant with it and knew what he wanted. He was a Scotsman and was an architect that I had come to know through my landscaping work. The project involved some quite heavy work and I had to re do quite a lot of the work involving some tile paving because I had difficulty with the levels. He was very particular about the curves to the shrub beds where it met the turf and I had to redo several of these several times, resting his patience and mine! Somehow, I managed to get the work completed. He was, surprisingly, unaware that I was drinking on the job. I would start drinking as soon as I left the house and often before he went to work, he would invite me to discuss the project and have a cup of coffee. I went to make amends some years later and it was then that I spoke of my drinking and he told me that he had been unaware. Despite my hard work, there were still a lot of defects and quite a few plant losses so another contract was drawn up to remedy things and the cost was deducted from my account.

I remember once when I was driving home with a tractor with a rotavator on the back, someone drove in front of me and there was no way, with my heavy load, that I could stop. The truck, not very valuable, was a write off. What surprised me is that I was not breathalised at the scene of the accident. If I had been tested then I surely would have been prosecuted and banned from driving. This would have cost me my business. The truck and trailer were taken back to the depot and I was given a lift back home. It was most inconvenient not having a truck and so I hired one until the replacement arrived.

During all of this, Marta must have become more than a little disappointed in me and frustrated by my selfish behaviour. I remember one evening, I was lying on the bed, no doubt a bit drunk, in the bedroom that we still shared. She quietly came into the room and placed the letters beside me that I had sent her while she was still in Bratislava quite a few years back. I knew what she meant by this act and I know that I had disappointed her but I was powerless, in the grip of this disease. I know that this is no excuse. My youngest daughter once wrote 'cut out the crap' on one of my gin bottles. I think she also poured my gin away and replaced it with water but this didn't deter me, I was consumed by the madness. I knew, five years or so before my last drink, that I was an alcoholic but I was never seriously challenged about it. I was totally irresponsible, giving driving lessons to our youngest while I was drunk too. On one occasion I was drinking early in the morning ready to drive up to York with the family for a break. When we approached the third roundabout in Milton Keynes, our middle daughter protested that unless someone else was going to drive, she would walk home[nr1]. Fair play to her and her sister. When we got to York I had 'the shakes' as I drank a cup of coffee. This was still a long time before my last drink. At one point, Marta suggested that I go to see my doctor but I refused, I guess I was too ashamed of myself. It was not long after that when she asked me to move down to the study where my mother used to sleep. I accepted this, I guess because it allowed me to drink more. Soon after this stopped showering, I was right in the thick of a nasty addiction. I had become a nuisance and this was my justification for drinking more. The old 'poor me' syndrome.

Going off on a tangent, I must relate the latter stages of my mum's life with Alzheimer's disease. I originally became aware of it when we were playing Cluedo with the family and she couldn't remember any of the people etc and we just laughed it off. Later on, she told us that she had found her neighbour dead on her doorstep and I believe that this was a trigger. As time went by, we visited her every two weeks or so and she was steadily becoming more confused. When I found rotten ham in her fridge, I decided that I had to do something about it and get her to come and live with us. That was obviously going to be very difficult in our already cramped conditions but Marta and the girls were very accepting of the situation. I informed the bank of her situation and they rightly closed her account. I opened another account for her affairs and got her to sign a

Power of Attorney. Of course, it was only a matter of time before I was stopped for drink driving. There were quite a few other embarrassing situations regarding my drinking, best not told here. It was my habit, by then, to go and do some work on my allotment because I didn't have much else to do. I would do some work there having been drinking most of the morning and then go shopping to a nearby Tesco. Mostly this was just to buy more booze to last me over the weekend and to fill up my truck with fuel. I must have been swigging from a gin bottle whilst on the forecourt of the garage and been seen by someone. The police were alerted and I was pulled over a couple of miles down the road. I was breathalised and taken to the local police station in hand cuffs. A humiliated man. I was obviously over the limit but not by much because I was a 'top up' drinker. I was released after three or four hours when I had sobered up. When I came out of the police station there was our youngest daughter and her boyfriend waiting to greet me, much to my shame. I guess they saw my problem and knew where I would end up. I went back to my truck and drove home. I knew then that I would lose my licence and what was left of my business. I made plans to sell all of mt landscaping equipment. The two tractors, trailer, rotavators, mowers and finally, my truck. They were sad and confusing times for me. I apologized to Marta but it was all just empty promises. I couldn't stop drinking. I desperately needed help but it was a long time coming because of my obstinacy. When I attended court, I was handed quite a heavy fine of £1000 and a driving ban of fifteen months. Things were so bad that when I attended a drink driving course early on Saturday mornings, I would board the bus with two bottles of gin and one of water. I would have a swig on the way, during breaks and all the way home. On one occasion, a fellow offender commented that I smelled of drink. I lied and said that I'd had too much the previous evening. Having lost my business, I had time to drink even more. Once, I walked two or three miles to my allotment and pretended to do some work, carrying my gin and juice along with me. I spent most of that time in the shed drinking and smoking. Otherwise, all I had to do was go down to the local convenience store to buy booze and cigarettes. At home I was drinking a combination of gin and red wine, still never getting a hangover. Often, I was in such a confused state that I could not remember the pin number for my bank card and was shaking as I walked to the local Tesco. On perhaps two occasions towards the end I had blackouts, fell in my bedroom and broke some drawers and sent the television flying. I also banged and cut my forehead leaving a scar close to my eye. Luckily, I was not wearing glasses. Like many alcoholics, I was putting my own life in danger and my wife and family were having to witness this. Not long before my last drink, I was supposed to go and visit my sister and her husband near Perth in Scotland. I had some sort of panic attack as Marta was taking me to the local railway station. I could not bear the thought of not being able to drink whilst going through boarding procedures. Marta rang my sister who said that they were aware that I had a problem with drink because they could smell drink on my breath in the morning and had seen all the bottles.

22 IS MY LUCKY NUMBER

Ever the bonny baby, my first picture and one a bit more up to date

MR HEDLEY KIRKMAN

Marta and myself enjoying sea and sun in Mexico.

My 70th birthday.

RECOVERY AND A NEW LIFE

About a month or so after I had failed to get to Scotland, my wife and family had seen enough ad had been concerned that I might fall and do myself serious injury. Marta consulted my doctor about me being taken into hospital but he seemed reluctant to help, talking about human rights?! What about my family's rights? They had suffered enough as had I. So, Marta, with the family's agreement, rang for an ambulance to take me to hospital on the 10th December 2009. This was for my own and their safety. For about three or four hours I refused to go and so the police were called. I was fearful about what might happen because my family and I had not always had good experiences at Milton Keynes hospital. I didn't become physical but I can be really obstinate in a situation like that. In the end their patience ran out and I was bound up and bundled into the ambulance. I was taken to A&E where I was put on a drip and assessed. Surprisingly, my thoughts were still clear and I realised that my time was up. I came to realise that this was my rock bottom. I had done enough damage to my family and to myself and I could not let them suffer any more because of my selfish behaviour. I was in a sorry state. I knew then that the only way out for me was to ask to be sectioned under the Mental health Act. I didn't know what it really meant other than it was for people with disturbed minds and I certainly had a disturbed mind. This was a harsh fact and the reality of where drink had taken me. Early that morning, two young doctors assessed me and agreed that I should be sectioned. I was then put into a wheelchair and taken across to Campbell House. I had three weeks there which was a very testing and painful time for me in my confused state. Not only that, it was a difficult time for Marta and anyone who visited me. My wife used to visit daily and our youngest occasionally and when she could. I suffered from awful panic attacks and isolated myself to such an extent that I had to be locked outside my room. An example of my panic attacks was, every time Marta came to visit, I would tell her that I only had two or three hours to live and after a few minutes of conversation I would disappear back into my room. The lack of empathy and understanding defies belief as they told my wife that she was obviously upsetting me and advised her not to visit again. She was not deterred by this, bless her. On another occasion, our youngest daughter asked me, 'Did you mean what you said that you wanted to be sectioned and you feel like a piece of shit?' I replied, 'Unfortunately, yes...' I had not eaten for so long, as I had purposely fasted for three weeks.

Marta continued to visit every week but, unbeknown to me, she had other plans for me, bless her. After three weeks I knew I had to move on, I had already outstayed my welcome. But where was I to go? I was still living in fear. It was in between Christmas and New Year and I knew the family had plans to be away in a cottage near Bath. I was not going to spoil the plans as I had done so many times before. My wide and daughters decided that I should go to rehab, although they didn't know what it involved. Our youngest searched the internet and found a load of places. I know that my wife made twenty-two phone calls on my behalf (another reason for the title of this book!) I needed to be in a safe place to recover. Marta made twenty-one calls one Tuesday evening and pledged to make just one more. If she wasn't successful, she planned to place me in a care home where our daughter had worked. In the event, this was not necessary. I said later on that it was like there was no room at the inn. The twenty second place that Marta phoned said, 'If your husband is brought here tomorrow with a few basics like clothes, he will be assessed. If he is thought suitable for treatment he will not have to go back home.' The rehab turned out to be the only one that was run by the Salvation Army. When the people at Campbell House found out about this, they took even less interest in me. Marta and pour middle daughter took me down to Highworth near Swindon one cold and foggy morning. Because I was so nervous, I talked incessantly all the way there. I was still extremely fragile. When I got there, I was quickly assessed and accepted. I was so unsteady on my feet that they feared I had 'wet brain' but somehow, by the Grace of God, I didn't. I was damaged mentally. I said goodbye to my family, shed a tear or two and my luggage was inspected. Some Lucozade that I had been given at Campbell House was returned to me as I was allowed energy drinks. I was given a room on the first floor that overlooked the patio area. I was really confused and disorientated and still having regular panic attacks and talking rubbish. I was advised by one of the key workers, to write down how I was feeling in my journal. I still keep a journal today and still have my first with that shaky writing to remind me of just how ill I was. Keeping a journal helps me to review my day and keep appointments. I was assigned a buddy to look after me which was a nice idea. When New Year's Eve arrived, I was told that everybody was going out to do some ten-pin bowling in nearby Swindon. I went into panic mode and said that I only had two or three hours to live and there was no way I was going. In the end I asked my buddy if he would take a mobile phone with him because if I did go, I might need to go to A&E. I was gently persuaded to go. They told me if I didn't go then nobody would. Of course, nothing happened and I survived the evening. I even had a good go at bowling.

I continued to have panic attacks and I remember one particular attack when I was attending a group session on a Monday in the front room. It is very difficult to explain but I had this attack and was allowed to go to my room to calm down. After an hour or so I came back and resumed my day as if nothing had happened. Nobody made any comment and I was treated kindly. The other problem I had was eating. As I had experienced ion Campbell House, I found it difficult to eat a square meal in my anxious condition. I used to drink lots of water so that when meal times came around I could not eat it all. This obviously upset the chef because he didn't like his food being wasted. Gradually things got better and I began to eat. I also had problems controlling my bodily functions but I could provide a sample in the mornings as required because that was the routine. One day I had the bright idea to provide my sample in a plastic cup that I had found in my room. I presented it to the staff in the office and they were not best pleased because it was completely unhygienic. Hygiene was not a huge priority for me at the time and I used to urinate into the hand basin at home, telling myself that I was saving water by not flushing the toilet. I often did it without washing my hands. One Scotsman there called me 'Clatty Clive' because of my lack of hygiene and my reluctance to change and wash my clothes. Alcoholism had made me lazy. A prank was played on me when they hid my dirty pullover behind the television. Slowly, slowly, things got better and after about one month I had put on a stone in weight, I was the lightest I had been in my whole adult life. I continued to take antidepressants and vitamins and every weekend we attended group sessions. We covered a whole range of topics about addictions and how to overcome them. I think around half of the clients were drug addicts. I enjoyed doing meditation and mindfulness sessions run by a very kind key worker. We also had peer groups where we could discuss each other's progress or lack of. They were honest and sometimes rather harsh we can't always see ourselves as others see us. But, perhaps more importantly, we were introduced to various fellowships and started to do the steps which we did one afternoon each week. My mind was still very foggy and confused and I had difficulty assimilating information but I did the best I could because I was desperate not to go down again. I knew that my life depended on it. We went to fellowship meetings every week, mostly Narcotics and Cocaine Anonymous but they all follow the same programme of recovery or 'the steps.' We were advised to look for similarities and not differences. I used to attend CA meetings until they closed down. One person who also attendee lost his life at quite a young age due to an overdose. When I last saw him, he looked well and healthy. When you relapsed after a period of being 'clean' you are very vulnerable.

I am sure we were encouraged and a few of us went to the local Methodist church where they were very supportive and friendly towards us. I got to know some of the congregation quite well. Weekends can be quiet a difficult time because there is not much to do and the mind can wander. Alcoholics and addicts need routine and for some of us it was a tough time. Later on, when I had started to get used to things, I would go for a walk or play snooker with some of the newcomers as that is when their sobriety can be tested. On Mondays we would have our weekly review of our progress, what we had been dloing over the previous week and our plans for the week ahead. We were also allocated a key worker to do a development plan. Somehow, the lady who I was allocated to completely forgot so I started a bit on my own. Once I had started it was useful and she became a good friend for a while. At the beginning when I was very shaky, she took me to do some shopping and to visit the local GP. We were also in the workshop on a Monday and Wednesday afternoon, which, to be honest, at the beginning, I did not like at all because I was so unwell. So, all that I was capable of doing were simple jigsaws that they had borrowed from a local; charity shop. I would complete all of this work with a bit of a grudge but would pretend to the staff that I was enjoying it. There was a lady that helped with pottery work which again I did begrudgingly.

One day I noted how clever one of mt fellow clients was and from then on, I had a complete change of heart. The other reason being that I realized that I could make items of pottery to give away when I left as gifts. From then on, they couldn't keep me away from the workshop and I even went to them to do extra time. In the end, I produced fifteen pieces of pottery and thirteen glass paintings. I gave all except two of these away over time. One of the paintings was of two field mice in a poppy field, I called the two mice Mickey and Marie and I gave it to the manager who happened to be my key worker. I still keep my pieces today, some nine and a half years later, out of gratitude.

After six weeks there I began to eat more normally and the grey drained look started to disappear, I still have evidence of that look today. I had two passport sized photos taken for a voluntary job application but I still looked pretty awful because I was still very thin. A photo was also taken of me with the manager, again I was pretending to be happy and I still looked gaunt in those early days. The amazing part about it was that the local press put it into their paper using my full name which I was sure they were asked not to do. The reason I found out was because when I went to the local fish and chip shop and mentioned my name, they said they already knew because they had seen it in the newspaper!

Then I got on to secondary, which not everyone did, after completing three months. I found it really helpful because it enabled me to re-engage with my family and the world at large. As an alcoholic, I had cut off everything including what was real or not. Even when in secondary, I did not behave appropriately and continued some old habits. I was being lazy one evening and slept in my day clothes and was found by a fellow client, much to his glee. I was rightly given a proper telling off from my key worker. In other ways in secondary, I became quite diligent and found myself three voluntary jobs, one working in a community café where my fellow workers were very friendly and patient with me. I also did the over sixties luncheon club close to the rehab where I did the washing up etc. Lastly, I worked in a local charity shop preparing clothes for sale where again, the manager and other volunteers were very kind to me. I was amazed one day when one of the volunteers asked me if I thought she was drinking too much. Yes, me!!

One thing that I have omitted to mention is from when I was still in primary, Marta came on her first visit after I had been there about three weeks. It was a Sunday and my key worker had been good enough to give up a couple of hours of her Sunday for us. The purpose of the meeting was to discuss how my drinking had affected the family and for me to make amends where appropriate. Marta was a little surprised when I brought a pen and paper to the meeting because I was determined to get things right. In the beginning, Marta spoke of the damage that I had done but I wasn't going to take all the blame. I wouldn't get well that way. I think the meeting went well and there was a general meeting of minds. Afterwards, we went for a meal at the local hotel. There were two other couples there, wine tasting and I just told myself that I thought I could enjoy life without a drink. On the whole, this has proved to be so.

Around this time, I decided to write to our two youngest daughters because they had been the most affected by my drinking. They were both good enough to send replies. The eldest one accepted my apologies and understood that I had an illness. The other one held a different perspective which I have to respect. She accepted my apology but went on to say That I should realise that I had damaged her for the rest of her life.

Throughout this time both in [primary and in secondary, I would have weekly meetings with my keyworker. I had a lot of respect for her, as I did for all of the staff. They worked very well as a team and brought different qualities to working in challenging situations. One lady was especially tolerant, she put up with quite a lot of abuse and was very good at running meditation sessions. Most of us were very sick in varying degrees when we arrived. I remember one guy who was severely jaundiced. After about three days he began to hallucinate and as I sat next to him in one session, he told me that there were bars up at the windows. I think it was that that caused him to run away and he was picked up by the police and taken to the local hospital where he escaped from the ward. He was found in the car park and returned to the ward. When he came back to the rehab, he completed the programme and, as far as I am aware, he is still sober today.

After a while, I was allocated to buddy a new man who had just arrived. He was profoundly disabled and, at the beginning, he was in a wheelchair. He also had a broken leg which had happened whilst he was drunk and been knocked over by some local yobs. I took it was quite an honour to look after him because I had never looked after a disabled person before. I was surprised when one of our fellow clients, who was quite arrogant, suggested that he was not so severely disabled and could walk up the stairs. No way!! Around this time, Marta visited me about three or four times and also our youngest daughter.

As my time at the rehab came to an end, there was quite a lot of lengthy discussions between myself and my key worker as to where I should go to live when I left. It was important to me to begin what was to be my new life and to stay sober. I was till lacking in confidence and fragile after six months. My wife was still drinking rather too much and moving back in with her was not really an option and I didn't fancy living in any other area of Milton Keynes. It would be easy to become isolated there and put my sobriety at risk. Isolation is one of the worst things for an alcoholic. I didn't have the use of a car at the time and a car is pretty much essential in Milton Keynes. Luton was mentioned but I had no desire to go there. Bedford therefore became the preferred option. I knew the place quite well having once had a girlfriend living there and of course, our girls went to school there. Also, the Salvation Army has a very active corps in Bedford so that became my preferred choice. One surprising incident happened when I went to Bedford to view a flat with Marta. As she parked the car and was putting her disabled badge in the window my ex-girlfriend appeared. She asked how I was and then, looking at Marta, said in a derogatory tone, 'Well, I see you have wife then?' I replied that I had and that we had a booking at a local restaurant so we couldn't stop and chat. During the meal and again later when we were doing some shopping, Marta, in her usual quiet way, chose to make no comment. I thanked her for that several times. Wes aw only one flat that was not very good but I was prepared to take it but Marta said no. She and our middle daughter found me a better one. One Sunday in midsummer, it was time to say my goodbyes to my fellow clients and one or two of the staff. I was out into the big wide world and away from the cocoon of rehab.

Friday had been my official leaving day and was also the annual open day. We had our usual meditation session and then I was invited to do what is called 'the three chairs' when you tell your story. You talk about how you came to be in rehab, your experiences and your hopes for the future. Hence the name 'the three chairs' because you moved from chair to chair as you spoke. I finished off with the prayer of St. Francis of Assisi which was well received. After a light lunch we began to prepare for the open day. Previous clients would be there as well as supporters of the rehab and various other people involved with recovery including social services and Salvation Army members. After eating some snacks, I became involved in a conversation with the personal assistant to a Baroness who supported the unit. As we strolled around the garden, I spoke of my experience of being in the rehab and she later introduced me to the baroness. She invited me and my wife for tea at the House of Lords, an offer we have never taken up although I have corresponded with her.

When I arrived in Bedford it was a Monday in midsummer. I stayed with family friends and I had to do this for two or three weeks because my chosen flat was not yet ready for me. The first thing I had to do was look at my mobile phone because it had developed a fault which I quickly resolved. My next call was to the SA Corps where I was made very welcome by the administrator, Kevin whose name I had been given. He was very friendly, showed me around the building as well as giving me a cup of tea. He became a wonderful mentor to me, endlessly encouraging me with various voluntary jobs.

In the evening I attended my very first AA meeting. It was within walking distance of the South Wing of Bedford hospital where the room was rented for the meetings. As it wasn't so far, I went on foot and I didn't have a car at that time although I had got my license back. It wasn't easy to find the room but after asking a lot of people I finally found the way. I was pretty desperate to get to the meeting because I didn't want my old life back again and would go to any lengths as they say. It was all still so fresh in my mind. Asking the way broke my anonymity but that did not worry me in such a situation. I was not and am not ashamed that I am an addict now that I have found recovery. For others, it may be different which I have to respect. Somehow, I found the meeting room and, to be honest, probably because of my nerves, I do not remember much about what was said but I do remember that I was made most welcome.

The following day there was a meeting at the SA at 1.30pm so I knew my way there alright. This one was a smaller meeting where I was to meet the man who became my first sponsor for two years or so. I can't remember much of what I did for the rest of the week except for Friday when I was set on at the local shop. I worked there for about eight years every Friday afternoon until something cropped up. I did the washing up and prepared potatoes for the following day, occasionally waiting at tables and using the till. I was given a free meal for my labour. Doing work in charity shops did not appeal to me because I thought I wouldn't be kept busy enough. After that I decided to keep myself busy by doing the week and gaining myself some experience.

As I may have mentioned, I used to visit these 'aunties' in their homes with my mum. They may have been widows or spinsters and also probably a bit lonely. We would visit them and have a cup of tea and a chat. My youngest daughter used to work in a care home for her work experience. She found it to be very rewarding and we, as a family, befriended a lady named Wynn and we used to take her to fetes etc as she was quite frail and wheelchair bound. This prompted me to volunteer in a local care home in Bedford. I applied for, and got, a DBS and visited to volunteer there for about four years. I got to know at least three of the residents quite well. I finally stopped visiting when the only friend that I had there decided that he didn't want to see me anymore. I thought I may have upset him but the fact was that he had developed a negative attitude to life.

Some time later, Kevin from the SA corps, suggested that I could do some waiting on tables at the over 60's club which I readily accepted due to my previous experience. I would also be able to socialize and share a free meal with them. It all worked well because straight after the club I could go upstairs and attend the AA meetings. Working at the over 60's club I got to hear about their aches and pains and of course, their lives. I got to know some of them really quite well.

One place where I attended an AA meeting on a Saturday was at the local wellbeing centre (MIND.) Over a period of time the staff there gave me lots of advice on a casual basis. They particularly gave me advice about my anxiety. I cannot remember how it came about but I started to hand out leaflets for them, initially on a Wednesday every two weeks. Later on, this became once a month because it was only the same information I was giving out in the leaflets. I asked if the colours of the leaflets could be changed every month so that it would attract people to notice them better. I enjoyed the walking and the engagement with people. I would go to various places including cafes, chemists, dentists, the job centre and the SA. Sometime after that I joined a peer group there and I found it most useful and we would share our experiences and activities of the week both good and not so good. In the end we were there to empathise and identify with other people's problems. I was also invited onto a course about how to engage with vulnerable people. Well, it proved to be much more than that. I learned about personal space, body language, eye contact and, perhaps most importantly, the ability to listen and how to ask open questions. After a while, Kevin asked if I would like to get involved in one or two other jobs. One was to be a receptionist for two hours every Thursday afternoon. I had previously spoken to someone who did that job and I thought that I could also do it. After a lot of initial training I became quite used to the job. It involved various tasks such as redirecting calls and it was this afternoon shift that also handed out food vouchers for the local food bank. They also gave out food parcels throughout the day. Sometimes it could be quite challenging because some of the clients obviously wouldn't be in a good mood. Some were suffering life's hardships or on drugs and the SA was the last hope for them because they had probably been to other agencies before that. A lot of them also had mental health issues. One other task I undertook as a volunteer for the SA was to socialize in what was known as 'open house.' There, people were given free refreshments and snacks. I was perhaps four or five years doing this task. On Sunday afternoons at 4pm they had what was called a SAMM, Sunday Afternoon Meal and Meeting, again for the homeless and lonely. I helped by waiting on tables, taking the desserts around and generally being helpful. I remember one Sunday when Kevin was there and a person completely 'lost the plot' due to a mental health condition. He hurled a chair across the room and everything went flying including a water glass, a jug and scattering glass everywhere. I was annoyed when Kevin took him gently by the arm and quietly led him from the room, sat on a wall and had a chat with him. I later learned that an ambulance had been called and he smashed up the hospital ward as well, ending up in prison. I know the man today and he is much calmer, I guess now his medications are working.

Occasionally, in winter, when the temperature was below freezing for a few days, I ran what was called the night café. Although I think night shelter better describes it and is financed by the local council using the SA facilities and premises. This is where the homeless came at abut 10pm, were given a meal, given blankets and bedded down for the night in the warmth. It can't have been very comfortable sleeping on the floor but netter than being outside. I would get home at about 8am and would carry on going about my daily business for the day before retiring to bed very early in the evening. It was nice to socialise with these people because they had lonely lives. It was also nice to chat with fellow volunteers unless they were always on their mobile phones which was sometimes their habit. There would always be about three of us for safety reasons. With all of these various nobs I was kept very busy, important to this alcoholic. I needed to be kept busy as I got bored easily and I liked it that way. Inactivity could be my worst enemy. Later in my recovery I began to overdo things and became mentally unwell.

At that time at the SA the AA meeting numbers began reducing so I used to put extra cash in the pot. It is much healthier number wise these days since it changed its venue. Another important aspect of a meeting is where we had a moment's silence to remember the still suffering alcoholics both inside and outside of the room. Sometimes I might pray for friends and relatives, especially my wife. Towards the end of the meeting we observe the yellow card which says 'who you see here, who you hear here, let it stay here.' At the end we say the Serenity Prayer together. At the first meeting I attended in Bedford I decided to make it my home group where you can hold various service positions such as being a welcome, serving refreshments, setting up the room secretary, literature secretary, treasurer and group service representation. I have held all of those positions over a period of time. Initially I did the refreshments and the washing up because this was an opportunity to do more with newcomers or a shyer person. Of course, I did not do these things on my own because it was quite a busy meeting with perhaps twenty or more people attending. Occasionally id get lazy and not go to a meeting as I should have done, making excuses about the weather or something that I needed to watch on the television. I also didn't tell anyone that I wouldn't be going. Selfish you might say. One evening they came to fetch me and from them on I became more diligent.

I also became more involved in the church. My first job was to be a welcome, handing out hymn books and taking the collection. I enrolled as a member of the church after doing a short course of induction based around our beliefs and then making my pledge in front of the whole congregation. For this I was given a lovely prayer book. I was asked if I would become a steward which was a role that was rotated once a month because there was three or four of us. It was a matter of helping to set up the service. I would make contact with the person who was to take the service and relay any information to the relevant people regarding the hymns and readings. On the Sunday I would arrive there a bit early, put up the hymn numbers and welcome the person who would be taking the service that day. We would them say a prayer together and I would thank everyone involved in the service such as the organist and then light the peace before handing over the service to the person to guide and preach. After the service I would take down the hymn numbers again and generally tidy up. After a while I stood down as a steward and became one of the churches representatives in outreach work, finances, property and safeguarding. Since I have found recovery, some wonderful and moving experiences have come my way.

A sponsor would usually be someone of the same sex who initially would go through 'The Big Book' with you and all the steps, in any way you prefer to do. Sometimes, you would need five pages of The Big Book each day, which is something I did recently. I have also done it by reading The Twelve Steps and The Twelve Traditions. I initially did the steps when I was first in rehab but, at that time, my brain was still somewhat scrambled so I was not able to do it to the best of my ability. We all got through different stages of recovery. Perhaps now, I am at stage two or three. I have now been approximately ten years sober. A few weeks after leaving the rehab I found my first sponsor. I had a temporary sponsor when coming to the end of rehab called Martin, he also had the nickname GBH, but actually, he wasn't as far as I was concerned. It would just be useful if I were to go off the rails! He had many years of sobriety and used to walk with a stick. When I arrived in Bedford, out of courtesy, I rang him to let him know that I was okay. I needed to give it serious consideration before I chose a sponsor in Bedford. After about a month or so, I identified someone and when I approached him, he readily accepted. This was someone who came to my notice who had some aspects that I admired. Not only did he have many years of sobriety but also seemed to be at great peace within himself and also a fabulous sense of humour. We began having a coffee after the Tuesday meeting, as we still do now just to socialise, and we got to know one another. We would discuss life and a bit about the AA stuff. Initially he came to visit me at my flat and later on I would go to his home. We spent a couple of hours doing a Big Book study and then began to do the steps. This was the first time after coming out of rehab. In rehab, my mind was very confused and so, when I came to steps four, five and six, I was rather disappointed in the man I chose (not my first choice) because he turned up late and then said he didn't have much time. After this, I managed to get the paperwork from the rehab which was very thorough and we gradually worked through it. I came to know that steps four, five and six are the life savers, or as some say, it sorts the men from the boys or the woman from the girls. In step four you make a thorough inventory of your misdemeanors to God, yourself and your sponsor. This consists of making a list of all the people you have harmed including organisations. We are then willing to make amends to them as in step nine, as long as it is not going to harm anyone. We would analyse our part, whether sloth, selfishness or pride and dishonesty etc. It is a matter of coming to terms with your past and to clear it out in an honest and responsible way. If we are not totally honest and open then we put our sobriety in jeopardy.

After I had completed step four, my sponsor suggested that I move on to steps five and six with a fellow AA member who I didn't like so much, nor he me. He was a longstanding member of the fellowship and we agreed to do it on a Thursday afternoon. I went through the procedure as honestly and as openly as I could and at step five, we prayed together for all of my character defects to be taken away. I am not the type of person who will get on his knees but I said the prayer with sincerity and something definitely worked for me. The rest of the day I spent as usual doing some reading and attending an AA meeting in the evening. The next day, something very strange happened which I can only describe as a spiritual experience. When I woke up on the Friday morning, I was completely devoid of energy although I had slept well. 'm not even sure whether I got up or made myself some breakfast but I do know that I just had a lazy day but not from choice. I was not so busy in those days so I had no commitments in the morning but in the afternoon, I was supposed to go and work at the café. I decided not to ring them and tell them id had a spiritual experience in case they thought I'd gone mad and call for the doctor or an ambulance. As far as I remember I spent the day doing absolutely nothing for perhaps the first time in my life. When I woke up on the Saturday morning, it was as though nothing had happened and I carried out my usual Saturday routines. The only explanation I have is that it was some sort of emotional response to doing the steps four, five and six. I had removed the baggage that was weighing me down. A lot of people doing the steps experience this and have what we term as a psychic change. All I know is that I think differently and am more at peace with myself. I could now live my life on life's terms and was given a new energy through God and the new things that I was able to do. I had a anew zest for life but then I became rather manic.

Whilst I was in rehab, one of the key workers asked me if I was doing my routine. I thought he was talking about washing and shaving etc but he wasn't. He went on to explain that it is good to make certain readings and progress before beginning your day, when you have some quiet time. Since he suggested this, I have not missed one morning doing this and that is perhaps the reason why I have remained sober for a long while now. Even when I occasionally go on holiday still do these readings discreetly so as not to disturb others, even when I'm on a plane or in a hotel. I will find a quiet place to do my readings. I find that it gives me a good start to the day and is the reason that I continue to do it. This alcoholic, needs and enjoys, routine. I have to be careful not to think about other things while I am doing my readings.

Our youngest daughter found her way to Al-anon on her own initiative because of the alcohol abuse in our family. Of course, I also got the Al-anon messages for meetings. We had joint Al-anon and AA meetings and also conventions. It has helped me to understand the consequences of my behaviour and how I can become a better individual. It has also helped me to deal with the situation with my wife when she has had too much to drink. The AA meetings take various forms but usually it is a 'share' meeting where a person can share their experiences, strength and hope. Or, as some say, 'as it was and how it is now'. Some talked about their abuse of substances alcohol in my case, called war stories by some, how they found recovery and how they are today. People are then encouraged to share in return. Prior to that there are various readings and at the end a voluntary contribution is made which we call tradition seven. This pays for the rent, refreshments, literature plus sending money to other groups to help the still suffering alcoholic. Other meetings may be a reading from the AA Big Book or The Daily Reflections. Others do readings from the long version of The Twelve

Steps and The Twelve Traditions, often called The Twelve by Twelve. In all of these meetings, people are invited to share their experiences. One other meeting is called 'At Step Eleven Meeting' where we have meditation to improve our conscious contact with God. It is not a religious programme but a spiritual one. Some people prefer to use the words' Higher Power' and therefore, it can be anything you want it to be.

I have been out of rehab for approaching ten years now and I still keep in touch with them, particularly my keyworker through the good and nor so good times. I do this partly through gratitude, but also to get advice on occasions. There is quite a lot of humour in our discussions and I can make my keyworker laugh. Laughter is a sign of recovery and we witness this at meetings and in rehab. I gave all the staff nicknames such as 'my mummy', 'aunt' and 'uncle' etc. One man I called 'Peter the Rock' because he was always there for you when things got a bit tough. I have written to all of the staff on occasion to talk about my experiences. Most rehabs offer after care. Sometimes I would go to the open day and on other occasions and on other occasions do a 'share' with the clients. When I do this, I see myself in them when I was in rehab. They are in the early days of recovery and not so well physically or mentally, just as I was. It also serves as a reminder of what I need to do to stay well and healthy.

Another experience for me was what I call an amazing reward for my sobriety, perhaps three years after I had come to Bedford. I had started day work as a receptionist at the Salvation Army corps. One Thursday as I arrived at work, on the table was a copy of The Salavationist which had my photo on the front! I was not aware that it had been used and nor did I give my permission but it didn't phase me. My experiences with the SA had always been good ones but the two new majors I thought, weren't up to the job. The lady became stressed easily and had to take time off work. The gentleman, for me, was not the 'real deal'. On one occasion I became involved with bim regarding the rent for the AA meeting which was which was to be increased quite drastically. This made it difficult because it was not a very big meeting at that time. He likened it to Tesco putting up their prices and then asked me what I thought. I said I would complain to the manager the same as I was doing with him right then. The rent had not been put up for some time so I agreed with that. I did not agree with the comparisons to Tesco. On another occasion, I was on reception and was the only one in the building. It was quite stressful because if someone arrived in a bad mood or under the influence of something, it could be very difficult to deal with. In fact, a pair of socks was thrown at me in the past, I was lucky that it wasn't a tin of food. On this occasion, two people had managed to get in at the same time and I was unable to stop them. When I finished my shift, the majors happened to be outside. I said that I was unhappy at being left on my own and he replied that I could just always keep the door closed. I did not think that that was the SA ethos and told them so. Lastly, I attended a talk run by youngsters and the topic was 'talking to God'. I happened to be sitting next to the major and our task was to describe our holiday experience and our favourite house and garden. After this we had to rest our hand on our neighbour's shoulder and talk to him or her through God. I did this firstly with the major, praying for him and his wife's good and for success as our majors. He then rested his hand on my shoulder and spoke these words, 'I see you standing by a cesspit and thinking of jumping in'. That was all he had to say. I was somewhat in shock as he knew. I was an alcoholic and felt like shit. I used to cry out those words. I thought his comment was unkind and insensitive and from then on, I stopped going to SA meetings. When I told mt key worker at the rehab she said that he was saying that God was testing me but I beg to differ. I don't think I needed or deserved, to hear that.

When it came to my family, those relationships improved although my wife can be hard work at times. Drinking causes us to harm our nearest and dearest the most. My family were a great help to me during my early recovery, finding a flat for me and getting it furnished. Marta has been quite a few times to England and to Scotland since she's been better; To the seaside, gardens, stately homes, the Lake District and National Trust Gardens. We also made two special trips to Mexico in the area of Cancun. To exotic resorts that were self-contained and all inclusive and were by the sea. They were set in lovely, landscaped surroundings with what they call 'drop down' and you could just swim down to the nearest pool and be brought refreshments as you swam. Of course, Marta enjoyed everything more than I did and was in her element. I am not a keen swimmer so I would walk alongside as she swam down. You could also lounge on the beach and have drinks brought to you. There were lovely tropical gardens where palm trees cast a shade for foliage and lots of flowering plants flourished. Marta loved it when we took bread from the breakfast and fed it to the fish in the sea. After finishing the bread, they would nibble at her foot and gave her a free pedicure! She also enjoyed the various massages on offer. Although it was now about one and a half years since I had last taken a drink, I was still rather fragile physically and not being a strong swimmer, found it quite hard work. We were taken out on a boat and did some snorkeling but Marta kept an eye on me. It was like the honeymoon that we never had, along with a few disappointments. We did have a bit of an argument and, as I do, I walked away and returned to our room where we met later. She said she thought id gone off to have a drink but, thanks to doing the fellowship, the thought never entered my head. I knew that would solve nothing. I couldn't blame her for thinking that a I had done it so many times in the past. As well as the trip to Mexico we had other but trips which improved our relationship.

The main challenge came on our second trip to Mexico. Marta was able to sleep on the plane but I hardly did. I was tired when we got to the resort and I soon fell asleep. When I woke the next morning, I thought that Marta looked a bit strange, but I didn't question her. When we went to leave for breakfast, she could hardly walk. She was totally drunk. I suggested that she went back to bed and I had breakfast on my own, rather an unhappy man. When I returned to the room, she was asleep and I looked around to see where the drinks were. It didn't take long and I found a line of spirits in one of the cupboards and I noticed one measure had already been partly drunk. I hid the bottles behind the curtains and later asked the staff to remove them. When she woke up, I told her that Id had the drink removed and her reply was, 'Well, that's good, you might be tempted to have a drink'. Denial. I then think I read something out of the Big Book and told her, without judgement, that I was not the problem, but that she had the problem and she unfortunately still has. What was really sad was that when she gave me her mobile phone, I noticed there were some pictures on it but didn't take much notice of them. When I mentioned it to her, she gave me a rather guilty look. So, I had another look and one photo showed our youngest daughter at the very same resort. I didn't mention it to Marta but when I had the chance, I mentioned it to our daughter. I thought maybe she had been there with her boyfriend and didn't want us to know. I discovered that she had been there with her mum and Marta had done exactly the same, getting totally drunk. This is the nature of the disease, we hurt our nearest and dearest. I have never mentioned it to Marta so as not to inflame the situation. I am aware of the Al-anon message, you didn't cause it, you can't control it and you can't cure it. As time went by, my relationship with my family improved, I have a very loving and forgiving family. I often say, 'I would not be the man I am today without my wife and lovely daughters'. On the other hand, there is a co-dependency between our youngest and her mum which is quite common in these situations. Its not surprising because she has never known her mum to be sober. Sometimes she can be strong and stand up to her mum. For instance, she had to choose where to be in order to continue her work as a junior doctor. Her mum asked her to study in Milton Keynes but our daughter decided to go to Cambridge which has higher standards. Due to the stress, she has developed irritable bowel syndrome and she has been on antidepressants at times and has also had to have counselling.

Now that I have become more reliable, hopefully I am now also a more conscientious husband again. Of course, I know that I'm far from perfect but at least I have learned through the AA programme that teaches us progress, not perfection. On one occasion, when I had been sober for a while, Marta went on a big binge at home. Our youngest daughter phoned and asked me to come over because Marta had fallen over in the kitchen and they were struggling to get her to bed. They thought they might need to take her to A&E because they were so worried as she has high blood pressure. It was a half hour drive for me and while driving I started worrying about what I might find when I got there. By half way there, I handed things over to God and felt quite calm. When I arrived, she was crying like a baby and we decided not to take her to hospital. There are a lot of similarities between our youngest and her mum, both being Pisceans and especially Marta as she is a proper fish, loving her swimming and having no concept of time. This reminds me of an amusing story about Marta although she may not agree. On our first visit to Mexico, we decided to take a taxi to a local beach although it was bot so good for swimming. I had a bit of a dip followed by a little sleep. When I looked up, I could see Marta was till in the sea and a fair way out. I then had a sunbathe and when I next looked up, she was gone. I walked down the beach in the direction that I thought the current may have taken her. After walking for half a kilometer or so, there she was, crying with her flippers in her arms. She then said, ' I thought I would never see you again'. Bless her!

It is often said that the spouse of an alcoholic views them as a child who is out of control and this can also be the case in early sobriety. All we want to do is go to meetings or so it appears to be. I experienced two things during my recovery which required my patience. I told my wife that I needed a car and she asked me why. I told her it was because I liked to go to meetings out of ton and could also give other people a lift, have a social life and visit my family in Milton Keynes. I don't think she understood because she didn't understand my need to attend meetings. I eventually got the car that I had bought for our youngest when she was attending school in Bedford for two or three days a week. She called the car 'Chrystal' and it was immaculate. I did have a laugh though because whenever she borrowed it and brought it back, there was virtually no petrol in the tank, but, more importantly, little oil in the engine. I forgave her for this as she was still in training and had a pretty hefty loan. After a while I suggested to Marta that I get a computer so that I could get on the internet and do AA business etc. Again, she was reluctant but, in the end, I got one and it has been an immense help to me, particularly of late.

As time has gone on, I have learned much in the Fellowship by doing service etc. With the twelve step programme we bring our character defects into check and concentrate on our talents which most alcoholics have in abundance. In this way we come to understand the mistakes we have made in our past particularly regarding our addictions. When we go to meetings we hear various stories of experiences, strength and hope. Perhaps, most important for me is that I am an addictive and compulsive character who can be rather self- serving which some may call greediness. The programme helps to control these issues. We may indulge in a lot of obsessions, two of mine being to smoke and I have a liking for too much sugar, chocolate and some may say, food in general. Although my diet is quite a lot healthier these days. We also tend to be quite Jekyll and Hyde characters, particularly when drinking. We may become argumentative or aggressive but I just used to fall asleep. Marta used to say, 'Clive, go to bed!' For others it can lead to marriage break ups, being hospitalised or sectioned and of course, being put in prison. Many of us are also shy, introvert and sensitive people who use substances to mask the way we feel. This is what I did when at parties, nightclubs or socialising in general. I remember going to a party, long before I became an alcoholic and then leaving the party because I hardly knew anyone and couldn't approach someone if I didn't know their name. I am somewhat different now.

And so it was, I was quite a lonely character before I married and also again when I found sobriety. We tend to be quite impatient people who don't take advice easily. Some three years ago I was diagnosed as being Bi-polar which explains why I have a variety of problems. Waiting in queues is a bit of a problem for me but I don't get up to any Mr Bean style tricks! We tend to be quite childish people and of course, drink stunts our spiritual and emotional growth. It is only once we stop drinking and join the Fellowship that we begin to grow up. We also tend to be worriers which causes anxiety and then the abuse of substances, even prescription drugs. This also led to depression for me on occasion. Once prior to my marriage and again when I became an alcoholic because drink makes you feel depressed, or worse, suicidal. We like to be appreciated and liked although some may deny it. Lastly, we tend to be risk takers and I certainly am as I have already related regarding playing with fire as a child and my abuse of alcohol as an adult. I have put my body through a lot of abuse and this has damaged my mental health. I still look quite young for my age, so people tell me and I am now seventy-one years old. We find it impossible to stop the damage we are doing to others and to ourselves. It is a drunken spiral that we have no control of. I believe that we are the blessed ones because we are able to carry the message to the still suffering alcoholic and that is a good way to stay sober as our co-founder and his wife do. The founders of Al-anon, what a legacy that is.

For a while I was doing seven or eight meetings each week and on Saturday's I would sometimes do three meetings. Obsessive compulsive behaviour! I have eased off somewhat now but believe that I need to do meetings for the rest of my life. In the

SA I continued to take on more commitments and became one of the main bus drivers. It didn't last long because I talked too much and it was thought that I was putting the passengers at risk. I reluctantly had to stand down. It was on a monthly rota where we picked up the old folk for the over 60's club and also for the SA meetings. Some of them would not have got there without this service. Obviously, on these occasions, I attended their meetings instead of going to the Methodist church. We would have refreshments after the meetings.

In my work life, I gradually took on more responsibility along the way besides the SA. This led to me having mental health problems. More on that later. It showed me the importance of building things up slowly and not over committing myself because I treat voluntary work as seriously as I treat paid employment. The church encouraged me to join 'Friends for Life' which co-ordinates the visiting of care homes within the Bedford area. For this, I needed a DBS but this made my life easier, any problems and I could consult with our co-ordinator. In the event, there have been no problems so far. It used to be that you had to be a Christian to join them but that's not the case now. The work gives me a lot of pleasure, just spending time with the old folks, hearing their stories and observing the lovely ways of their carers. I'm only there for half an hour or so and don't have to put up with their demands, moans and groans for too long! In the original care home, I met a Zimbabwean whose name was Tilsi which means compassion. What an appropriate name she had for a carer. The visits allow the old folk to talk about their lives and show their photos and many have interesting stories to tell. Of course, anything of a personal nature I don't encourage but if it should occur, it remains a secret and I adhere to confidentiality. Some of their stories may be of interest...

Ted, a man I the original care home that I volunteered at, lost his wife so went down to the local river to throw himself in. He could not swim. He looked back at his dog and changed his mind. He loved to talk about Liverpool football club.

Another gentleman was behaving inappropriately around the female care staff and had to be threatened with eviction. He told me this and that he had to stop it. Fortunately, he did and spent the rest of his life there.

A gentleman named Cliff belonged to the Plymouth Brethren and was quite a shy man but we swapped life stories, mine not as long as his. He again lived out his life in that home.

A bedridden man with dementia was another one that I befriended and at best, I could only get a grunt of a response from him. I spoke to the manager and said that I thought I was wasting my time and she told me it wasn't so, he was always more cheerful after my visits. After that I found a book about railway locomotives and read that to him because it was one of his interests.

My friendship with Charles developed into a special experience that I think makes for a nice story. He and bis daughter beckoned me over so I told them I'd like to befriend him and he seemed delighted. It must be very lonely in a care home and every day must seem the same, being confined to your room must surely be worse. Charles was blind so I was in a bit of a quandary with what to do with him. But, with a bit of good luck, I had a lovely, well researched book about Thomas Moore that I had bought for pennies at a local charity shop. I started too read a chapter to him at each visit which he seemed to enjoy and I forgave him for falling asleep sometimes! I was also drawn to the book because 'A Man For All Seasons' had been one of my favourites. As time went by. Although it was a big book, I managed to read it from cover to cover before he sadly passed away. I was invited to his funeral but unfortunately, the eulogy was not very enlightening because it was read by a lady from the funeral company. He was a dearly loved man and the manager and some of the carers cried at the service. I only ever go to funerals when I'm invited to by the family.

A memorable experience I had, occurred when I had been to a workshop at a care home about dementia. We were told that blue was the colour adopted by the dementia society and for-get-me- nots were their logo. Not long after this, Marta, who is good at flower arranging, produced an arrangement for me. In all innocence, she had used forget-me- nots and placed a blue candle in the middle. For me, this was God telling me that I was doing the right thing in visiting care homes.

Lastly, I began doing gardening work with fellow service users at the wellbeing centre. It was very therapeutic but I nio longer do it as much due to time restraints and a lack of energy, although it was a nice social activity. We are able to produce fruit, flowers and vegetables to take home for family and friends.

FAITH, RECOVERY AND SOME MISTAKES

As time had gone by, I have to admit to making some mistakes which affected my mental health and general well-being. In fact, some of these things could have led me back to drink. How it never happened I don't know because I was taking a big risk but then, I have always been a risk taker. Perhaps for about two years I maintained an honest AA programme but then I succumbed to temptation. I got involved with a lady and she was a serious alcoholic and I fell in love with her. I was told by at least two people not to get involved with her but, again, I was obstinate. She manipulated a lot of money out of me and, although I realized at the time that I was facilitating her, my love for her made me blind. After about two years or so, she died of an overdose or heart attack. Unfortunately, I wasn't informed in time and could not attend her funeral.

My second mistake was to start to pick up partly drank alcohol on the streets of Bedford. I would term this as odd behaviour... I did this for about a year or so and was asked to leave The Street Angels because I was seen doing it. The Street Angels in Bedford go out on a Saturday night to help people who end up worse for wear on drink and drugs. It was only when an AA member challenged me because he had seen me picking up drink, that I stopped. How I never got the craving back is still a mystery to me but now I know that I was dicing with death and that is the reality of it. Also, at about this time, I realised that I was becoming quite manic but I could not control it. It was an AA member who suggested that I see my doctor and she would come with me if it was an afternoon appointment. As it was, I was offered a morning appointment and decided to go for that. I have had some sort of recovery form this mania but it has been far from easy. I began to see various psychiatrists and my wife and youngest daughter have been very helpful. One thing that had been going on for quite some time was that I was behaving inappropriately at AA meetings, particularly with regard to women. Initially I was in denial about this but have now come to terms with it. I was accused of grooming ladies at the meetings but that was just not the case. I did fall in love with one lady at AA but when I sent her a text message, she told me to get lost. I also took alcohol addicts to at least two meetings and we behaved inappropriately. I guess, once again, this may have been perceived as grooming. I knew that my behaviour was inappropriate but I have seen and been told about worse cases although that is no excuse for myself. I became the topic of gossip which I never wanted and I was suspended from three meetings in Bedford. I was devastated and confused and so I rang the rehab and spoke to my sponsor. It was so bad that I sat and cried in my car when I was first told about one meeting. It was made worse because this lady told me I was a very sick man. That may have been so but it wasn't a helpful remark. It was so bad that one member came especially to a meeting to confront me physically. Ironically, a lady came between us so punches were not thrown. I say that he came especially because, in fact, he never usually attended that meeting. Now, some three years or more later, I have been accepted to meetings in Bedford except for one which I believe is unacceptable because it does not observe the AA tradition that its primary purpose is to help the alcoholic. Nowadays, it does not trouble me so much because I started to go to meetings outside of Bedford and have a new home group where they are very supportive of me and I now take on other service positions. As well as being a rotary secretary, I am also group service representative and represent our intergroup at regional meetings. I have accepted advice and hopefully improved my behaviour. I try to put a glass wall between myself and other members, particularly ladies, and I keep my hands behind my back. I am careful about the end of meetings as we hold hands to say the prayer. If a new lady member arrives, I exchange names and introduce her to other female members. I was also perceived by our Minister as behaving inappropriately but I think a lot of it is not true and are a matter of gossip mongering although I am not totally in denial. I stood down as a church steward but am still a welcomer. With regard to the gossip, I was accused of asking a lady if she was married and where she lived but none of which I believe to be true. Now I meet with the church superintendent every three months or so to review my behaviour which I appreciate.

Now, some five years later, I don't write as many letters to the rehab but I keep in touch by phoning my family regularly. Since I had a lull in my letter writing I thought it might be quite therapeutic to write my life story and to share my experiences, both good and not so good. Intend to be a creature of habit and routine, especially as I grow older. This tends to render me quite inflexible. I am, as already mentioned, an addictive and obsessive character, not just with regard to drink, but in life in general. One obsession is that I have to be on time for appointments and always have to have enough in store food wise so a lot of things go to waste. This was also the case with my landscape business and my finances.

My diet has changed somewhat and I do not eat so much but try to eat healthily. For instance, for breakfast I have various fruits and cereal with milk plus a helping of yoghurt. I used to never eat lunch but I do nowadays. I often have a light supper before going to bed and occasionally cheese, if I want to have some dreams! I guess I'm still a bit crazy. This brings to mind one dream that I had in sobriety. Like any alcoholic or addict, I had considered suicide and one plan was to place myself on a railway line that was near our house. I dreamed that I had gone to commit suicide and had placed my head on the railway line. As the train approached I rolled out of its way and found myself on the floor beside my bed after knocking my head on the bedside table.

With AA, I continued to go to six or seven meetings each week but now I only do four or so. Recently, I bought a t-shirt from one of the members which has 'I inspire others to recovery' on the front. I wear this to meetings on the fiber days. I think it is a privilege to wear it.

As aforementioned, I befriended an alcoholic/addict who led me to have an obsession with women and sex. Even now, my excuse is that I haven't been intimate with Marta for five years or more and I feel lucky to still have her as my wife because I do love her. Our relationship has changed somewhat, she has mellowed with age as I probably have too. She is not as critical as she used to be which makes life easier and I am able to introduce humour into our relationship. I gave her the nickname 'Ish' because she is invariably late when she agrees to meet or visit me. I asked if she minded but she said that it wasn't a problem. I call our youngest daughter Fish because she is a Pisces but not as Piscean as Marta. I have a special friend in the Fellowship whose name is Trish and I call them my three best wishes.

Marta and our daughter are aware of my inappropriate sexual behaviour but only in general and not in detail and I am surprised that they have anything to do with me. Marta in particular was devastated about my behaviour and they said they wouldn't tell our eldest daughter but, in fact, later they did. My psychiatrist and GP are aware of things because I have to be honest if I'm going to get better. I am now on medication to reduce my mood swings and I think it also reduces my libido. Early on, my local psychiatrist couldn't understand my condition so referred me to a professor at Addenbrooks hospital in Cambridge where our daughter trains as a junior doctor. I would visit her sometimes when I was there. The professor was very thorough and after an interview and discussion, he sent me for a brain scan and a long term memory test which took quite a lot of organising. He was extremely kind to me and asked me for my life story. I could hardly do that, being sixty-nine years old at the time. So I gave him a brief resume, of course talking about my alcohol abuse and he was also aware of my recent difficulties. After all of this, his comment was that I seemed to be a caring man.

The memory test lasted for a couple of hours or so and was quite intense. At the end, the doctor told me that she would inform the professor that I did not have a memory problem which was reassuring. The MRI revealed, in short, that my brain had been what I call pickled, by my alcohol abuse. The professor described it as my brain being older than it should have been. I believe that my alcohol addiction has exaggerated my mental health issues and nobody has ever contradicted that opinion. After this, he discharged me, saying I didn't need to see him again unless things deteriorated. It hasn't been necessary so far. I said a few emotional goodbyes. These are some of the reasons for the problems I was having but I don't use it as an excuse. If I do that then I won't get better.

Eventually, Marta and my family came to know that I was unfaithful when she found a used condom in my flat. As is her quiet way, she just left it on the kitchen worktop without a note. She had found it while she was tidying up. However, it did not affect my obsessions or bad behaviour. The state of me being completely out of control lasted about six months or maybe more, and I suppose it was Marta who first realised that things were out of control. My behaviour was completely disrespectful and unacceptable. I knew that I couldn't carry on like this or I would lose everything and end up homeless. I was allocated a counsellor volunteer through the wellbeing centre to help with my finances which proved helpful. Due to my debts I could have taken the easier route and declared myself bankrupt but I decided to engage with a charity called Step Change and I'm slowly paying off my debts. Over a period of time I have had allsorts of immediate debts including rent, council tax, water and electricity. I had become lazy and stopped looking after myself and my flat.

Despite all of this, I gave a pound or two to the homeless once in a while. I have recently discovered that some of them are not homeless but I try not to be judgemental. Some have mental health issues, suffered trauma, relationship break ups and addiction. Even if I don't give money to them, I like to give encouragement. I do this because there's always someone else who is worse off than me. I hope, as a consequence of this, and leading a generally active life, mostly good things will come to pass for me. I have lots of friends in Bedford and the surrounding areas and of course, my AA friends. It is not the number of friends but the quality. At my last check, I had over two hundred and forty friends on my mobile and of course, I have other friends whose phone numbers I don't have. Having a sense of humour helps. When I was drinking I didn't have a friend in the world because I disliked myself. With all of the walking I do, I see friends on a regular basis and it also helps me to sleep. I have very good friends in the SA, the church, the fellowship, care homes and of course, my lovely family and rehab friends.

I am on two Medications that I take in the morning which are basically mood stabilisers. These days my finances are somewhat better but there's still a long way to go because I still have substantial debts.

For quite a long time there was a question mark as to whether I have bipolar or not. The first psychiatrist asked me to describe my lifestyle and pastimes and, based on that information, concluded that I do not have bipolar. However, the question mark has remained. After about six months they did decide I have bipolar. Having attended some bipolar meetings I now realise that I have probably had this condition for most of my life. They explain why things have gone wrong and still do. Primarily caused by my anxiety and compulsive, obsessive behaviour, add to this being a slow learner and somewhat obstinate.

Because of the manic way that I ran my landscape business I burnt myself out. This led to my anxiety and severe depression. When it came to my marriage I did similar things, putting my heart and soul into it, then being disappointed. Partly because I was over sensitive and immature in my behaviour. These mental health issues have re-occurred.

Despite these various problems I am quite a determined person. I set out on a project and can show some patience. I always know that there will be light at the end of the tunnel, but often become confused about things. Fortunately, I have not become depressed of late. There are a few reasons for this. I receive immense support wherever I go, particularly from my family, the SA, the rehab, AA, church and, of course, my various doctors. Throughout my life I have had people helping me along the way but I also have a determination. I like a challenge, my marriage, my business and my recovery from addiction, despite the mistakes along the way. Perhaps my recent problems are the greatest in my life so far. I partly put that down to being a slow learner. I have been on some adventures, travelling and working in North America and Zambia. When I came back to the UK, gaining work experience and setting up a new business took much longer than I anticipated but it was all worth it. My next challenge was to get married to a lovely Slovakian with her three daughters who I was privileged to help bring up. The problem that Marta and I have with alcohol has not made life easy for any of us and it has tested our marriage. I know that I still love her but it is a different kind of love now that is difficult for me to explain. I have developed a greater sense of humour and Marta has mellowed somewhat which has made life easier. Of course, I do miss the intimacy. It is a bit of a miracle that our love has survived but, I feel that I only want to be married once. It can be hard work but is worth every minute. Today, with my alcoholism, my sister and brother in law have been very supportive and came to visit me when I was in rehab, coming all the way from Scotland. They are also aware of Marta's problems but can't help her like me. I haven't told my sister of my latest problems because I am so ashamed and confused.

Speaking of obsessions, my OCD seems to get worse as I get older. Some of it may be due to the bipolar as I now have a habit of making sure that things are straight etc. The way I obsess about some things makes life a bit harder than it needs to be sometimes. I also get a bit agitated when I'm stuck in queues etc but not nearly as bad as some people. I often arrive at appointments early due to my time obsession and I even obsess about keeping a diary, even writing down how many times I go to the toilet. It's no wonder I'm so busy! I now obsess about being on Facebook and have to check it on a regular basis but I'm careful about what I post on there. In all of this, as with AA, I can share my experience with others and, perhaps, help them. Despite these difficulties, I generally have a positive attitude towards life.

As I write this, I believe, through God and the fellowship programme, I am generally able to maintain my positive outlook on life. Having people around me helps, too many to list, but I must mention Marta and our daughters.

As previously mentioned, I get bored easily, surprisingly even now I am older. I have a lot of the traits of ADHD. I can be attention seeking and hyperactive which sometimes causes me to lack concentration and lose my thoughts. This could equally be due to my bipolar condition and why I need mood stabilisation medication. I will be checking my world incessantly as though wishing my life away. At one point, I was reading two or more books a day and in the end I was only scanning them. Consequently, I hardly read except for AA and social material. I was a regular visitor to the library where I found the staff most helpful. I prefer books that are educational such as biographies, history, politics and so on. I continue to have anxiety as much as ever in my life and sometimes find myself dry retching. Part of this is due to negative thoughts at the beginning of the day but I have a new mantra 'If yesterday was alright, then probably tomorrow will be okay too. If yesterday was not so good, tomorrow should be better '. Also, during any difficulties, I allow God to guide me through my day and that too makes life easier. So, why do I do this? Almost without exception, my days go Well and often better than expected. But, my character traits make life less enjoyable than it should be.

One way my anxiety manifests itself is a scratching spot that has developed on my right cheek. It started about four years ago with me thinking that I'd developed a nasty case of dandruff. This spread to all areas where there are hairs and caused me to develop a bald spot in the middle of my head. I knew it could get better because the hair follicles still remained. Eventually, after a lot of toing and froing, I was referred to doctors at the Royal

London hospital. The man in charge deferred me to one of his team. My first visit was an absolute disaster. I went with Marta and we travelled up the night before because it was a very early appointment. We took advantage of the situation and went to the theatre. When we arrived at the clinic, I saw the doctor's name from my letter up on the board so thought there'd be no problems. After watching for half an hour or so, I approached the receptionist, only to be told that he was not on duty that day. I lost my temper which I think I had every right to do but chose not to swear in a public area. I was referred to another doctor who was completely inappropriate because his speciality was ulcers. He suggested that I make a formal complaint. This I did, explaining the expenses that we had incurred and finally received a refund of £12 that no way covered the cost. On leaving I apologised to the receptionist but she said it wasn't a problem. When I visited subsequently, I always got a smile from her.

I was the first patient for the doctor that I was allocated to as I found out, because his inexperience was quite obvious. At one point, we were to do meditation but there was so much noise from outside, the session had to be abandoned. Another wasted trip. At the next visit, there was again noise coming from outside, so I suggested that the doctor play some relaxing background music. He said he'd do this on his mobile phone. After that I was asked to keep a diary of my scratching habit. Almost immediately I became lazy about keeping the diary and I relapsed. I still have the scratching spot but my hair has fortunately grown back. On one other visit, I got into a discussion with a couple of other patients in the waiting room. A young lad had extreme dandruff like snow which caused him terrible embarrassment. Another patient told him that he should just be embarrassed and stop taking his medication. What an ignorant comment!! Later, I was told that some of the people were on such strong medication that it gives them permanent liver damage but, what choice do they have?

A while ago, I had my worst day of anxiety since I was in rehab. I don't fully understand why this happens but I have some ideas. I drink copious amounts of water which, in turn, makes me need to go to the toilet a lot. I know that drinking water is healthy but I also know that the amount I drink is over the top. There is no way I'd consider drinking alcohol because I know that would be a worse move. I was not depressed but I was worried and concerned about my debts. Even writing this down is therapeutic and helps me to keep in the moment. At this point I had taken the health part out of my Power of Attorney and my cheque to the solicitor had embarrassingly bounced. He didn't seem too put out.

Now, I would like to write a little bit about my family and Marta who mean so much to me and, on the whole, had been so good to me when I was suffering with alcoholism and during my recovery, as was our youngest daughter. Marta was also good to my mum when she developed alzheimers and received little thanks. My mum hardly thanked her and upset her by making unkind remarks which upset Marta who is a sensitive lady. Our eldest daughter is very intelligent and went to Bedford and Cambridge. She seems to acquire knowledge like blotting paper so she doesn't have to work so hard. She now works for the EU in Brussels and attends the World Trade. Consequently, her life is quite stressful. She is married with two daughters. She was not supposed to have been told about my latest misdemeanours, however, Marta did tell her and she is rightly angry. We had some communication on her birthday but I have heard nothing since, some six months later.

Next is our middle daughter. She is the quiet one although she has come out of her shell a bit more of late. She worked hard and went to Bath University where she studied European Studies and Russian. As part of her studies, she did go to Russia which was a testing experience for her. She now works for the Open University and lives in Milton Keynes with her boyfriend. She lives quite close to her mum and looks after our rabbit and two cats. She is a very diligent and hard working lady but gets a bit stressed sometimes.

And so to our youngest daughter, who I have spoken about before. She is the one who I have given permission to be in touch with my psychiatrist and GP regarding my health and well-being. She is training to be a junior doctor and plans to become a GP herself soon. I have immense respect for her as I do for my other two for various reasons. Marta is very supportive of me as is our youngest daughter and I call her my mentor. Marta checks my bank account situation online and often comments on my erratic spending because, as well as my other problems, I have become a bit of a shopaholic. This has been a new incentive for me since I moved into my new flat over two and a half years ago. I now live in sheltered accommodation with a housing association. Marta continues to check on me and the state of my flat and encourages me to keep it tidy because I can be a bit lazy in this area. My old flat was with a private landlord who typically didn't want to invest and keep the flat up to date. The old flat ended up in a real mess because I was too lazy and untidy. I was allocated a care worker through the Senior Person's Mental Health Team (SPMH) and she was quite strict with me and set me targets. Again, my wife helped without a word of complaint. My youngest daughter also asked me not to smoke in my new flat which I have obeyed. I did smoke in the old flat although I wasn't supposed to. I leaned outside the bedroom window and managed to burn some holes in the carpet.

As time has gone by, I have become a bit of a hoarder using the phrase 'beware what you throw away' as an excuse. For a while it was getting worse but now I'm in my new flat, I do try harder to be more tidy. Part of this is my obsession collecting food books and making sure my mobile phone and tablet are charged up. These are not necessarily bad things but having these obsessions makes it difficult to relax and sometimes gives me negative thoughts. I also obsess about having enough petrol in the car and having oil in the engine. I worried about having enough money in my retirement and if I hadn't wasted money on my addictions, I would be quite secure financially. I have no savings, just debt. A while ago I had £27,000 in my savings account. I am determined to overcome this with the help of Step Change. I know I won't have a peaceful life until these things are resolved. But, it's early days yet, a peaceful life means, to me, fewer worries.

Since being in rehab, I have kept a diary every day as I was advised to do. I write in an abbreviated form. It records all the people I meet and the things I do. I find it very therapeutic as I do writing this tale. A diary also helps me to organise my life and keep my appointments.

FURTHER RECOVERY AND VOLUNTARY WORK

I love to continue to visit care homes and for a good while I was visiting three of them. I have now cut back to two. It is still voluntary work that I love the most and it is fortunate they are within walking distance from my flat. After some time, I have become a member of the Alzheimers and Dementia Societies. For the Alzheimers I have become a local fundraiser and I have done two 'Elvis days' which were a lot of fun. My family used to say that I was like an elf from The Hobbit after I had a haircut and due to my big ears! On the first occasion, Marta cut my hair in one of the care homes where I was sponsored to raise money. I made jokes about a certain Spanish bank who supports various charities including the Alzheimers Society. My saying was, 'open a bank account with them and you'll have an 'elvier' savings account!'

Once, while on a course, they asked me to talk about my experiences visiting care homes and of course I had to talk about Elvis day. Volunteering in care homes and attending some of the resident's funerals has been a very special and moving experience for me. Another was when the coordinator from Friends For Life told me that she had a new gentleman for me to befriend in a care home that I was already visiting. She happened to mention that he came from the local SA and when she told me his name, I already knew him. He was a Colonel and he had done a lot of missionary work with his wife in East Africa. I had met him and his wife through the over 60's club. It was quite apparent that he had dementia and often became confused and angry. He was transferred to another, more appropriate care facility where he sadly passed away.

At this same care home I noticed another man in a wheelchair who had suffered a stroke and I thought it would be nice to befriend him. He told me he had lost his wife, also through a stroke and had started to neglect himself. This is why his son got him into the care home. He has now improved because he exercises a lot and is no longer wheelchair bound. He is a Christian man who loves his golf. He is also a very caring man with a good lady friend and every day he does his exercises. A very determined man. In the long term he is hoping to be well enough to return home.

Some time ago, I became involved with dementia workshops and I found it most useful to hear what the tutors said about carers and befrienders. I also had something to bring to the table because of my experience with mum's alzheimers. I learned to live with someone with dementia. It can affect you in many ways and make you unwell when you're trying to do too much. It's important to look after yourself and have some respite sometimes. One lady whose husband had Parkinson's disease said that she felt guilty about placing her husband in a care home. Hopefully, being at the workshop, she would come to terms with this. With regards to myself, I receive help for my anxiety from many quarters but mostly these days through the SPMH team. I also attend workshops at the Recovery College here in Bedford sometimes. I don't see my doctors often enough due to them being overworked. However, I didn't give up and contacted my local MP's office to ask if they could help me out. My MP is interested in this area because he has at least one family member who has a mental health issue. I know that I have to engage with these people to gain long term recovery from my addictions and poor mental health. Connected to this, I attend quite a few workshops and meetings through Mind. The meetings are called peer groups, once a week, sometimes single sex and sometimes mixed. I prefer the latter because you gain a woman's perspective. Generally, we share our previous experiences and try to help each other. At one or two meetings I was encouraged to be a facilitator due to illness or holidays. I treated the meetings just the same way as any other and it seemed to go well. Once a month I go to bipolar meetings which are run in a similar way.

More recently, I have begun going to another peer group which is called a Spiritual Recovery Peer Group. In many ways, it is like the other groups except that we begin with fifteen minutes of guided meditation. After this we discuss the spiritual side of our recovery which often leads to some interesting discussions.

On one occasion I went to see my psychiatrist. I put myself through health checks before I went in to see her and was somewhat surprised to hear that my blood pressure was quite low. When I went into the room I showed her the slip and she immediately asked me if I was eating a proper breakfast in the morning. I replied that I was being lazy and wasn't. I have now mended my ways and weigh as much now as I have in my life. This particular doctor is very considerate and patient towards me, with a lovely sense of humour and always smiling. I see another psychiatrist who is not quite as cheerful. I always look forward to these appointments with these doctors, including my GP, as they are always good.

About three and a half years ago now, I began a small paid job delivering junk mail to various estates around Bedford and one or two neighbouring villages. It was quite strenuous work for this old man so I gave it up. I was lucky because although I did it over a winter, I only once got wet! I mostly used to do it on a Saturday because I am quite busy during the week. I tried to socialise with people along the way and took photos of plants in people's front gardens. It relieved the loneliness and I'm surprised at what lovely photos I have.

Speaking of plants and gardening, after searching for an opportunity in care homes, two chances arose in the space of a week. One was in a care home where I visit already and was organised by the activities lady, we are hoping to get some of the residents involved. It is in a raised area where the soil isn't so good but we found a few barrow loads of soil to improve the area to grow a few vegetables. It only involves half an hour to an hour or so but hasn't been much of a success because the residents have rarely got involved. Because I only visit once a week, the lack of watering has been a problem.

The second one is in the grounds of the wellbeing centre and there are quite a few people involved and there is also a facilitator who is a very nice lady. To be honest, I haven't done much because I always seem to be in a hurry. Prior to this it had been suggested that I do the work on a Tuesday but that is one of my busy days so I had to decline again.

Now to some of my obsessions and compulsions, my anxiety and manic behaviour all being a part of this. I usually go to bed around 10pm unless I go to an AA meeting. I'm usually up by around 5am, make a cup of tea, then I sit, scratching and reading.

On a positive note, I do my AA readings because that is the best and quietest time for me. Scratching and reading were a part of my day for many years but I have since cut back on reading and hardly read at all. I was starting to only scan books, reading two or three every day. Crazy. All of this anxiety I have had for many years and it gives me excretion problems. I remember many years ago, I soiled my pants when I was with my mum. It also happened once in Bratislava when I went to meet Marta and a friend. I managed to clean myself up. It still sometimes happens now, in Bedford but I obviously try to avoid it. I try to predict when I will need the loo, but I'm not always successful.

These days I have an obsession with women and I now realise that it's an obsession I've had since being young. The medication has helped me to slow down but not much so I'm able to prioritise and am not so confused. Although I wasn't given tablets to lower my libido, it appears to have been the case to some extent. I have to realise that it's a waste of time wondering if these prostitutes want my love and to be serious with me. Like many men, I seek their company because I am lonely. My wife, fairly recently, hinted that she has a boyfriend but now I believe she was teasing me. I don't tell her that I love her but I call her an angel for the way she still helps me. It would be inappropriate for me to tell her I love her because I misbehave so much and she knows quite a bit about it. I love her in a different way now because I still like her character and values and of course, the things that she does for me. I buy her little presents once in a while. I also have gratitude for the lovely daughters we have. I believe that all of these things are God given. I don't think that I would be alive today if it wasn't for them, or at least, I'd be totally mad. They are the ones who sought help for me. Even with family around me I was isolating myself and did not have a friend in the world, including myself. Because of my estrangement from my wife, I used to look on the Internet for a girlfriend or partner. I found one lady aged fifty-one who had surprisingly not been married, although she seemed very attractive to me.

We have only communicated so far on the Internet but she has many similarities to Marta. In fact, it came to nothing. Perhaps, due to some unhealthy relationships she alluded to. As a result, she was insecure about engaging with anyone. When we talked, she seemed to back off and then she said she was only happy to communicate through the website. I decided that this was a waste of time, especially since you have to pay for every message and I soon ran out of credit. For these reasons I had to give up on her.

After a while, I considered doing VSO again. I knew I'd have to be very wary about AA meetings and working on the programme. I also had to think about the impact of convincing Marta and our daughters although they are now adults. They may think that I was abandoning them after they have done so much for me in my recovery etc. In the end, it came to nothing because the psychiatric professor said it would be too much regarding my mental health and the availability of my medication.

Unfortunately, on one occasion, Marta got very upset with me and was in the worst mood I had ever seen her in. I did understand because it was about my selfish sexual conduct during the previous year or so. Unfortunately, I cannot change the past, equally, I could not give her any excuses she'd accept. However, on occasions, I would convince myself that it was all okay. She needs a loving and loyal friend and I have to understand if she finds someone else. I shouldn't be overly surprised, but it may never happen.

I am especially lonely in the evenings and overnight. I just want someone to share with and hear about their day, not to investigate, just to be interested in someone. Here I was, in July 2017, just turned sixty-nine years old and on the Internet looking for a partner. I never had any success. I told my rehab keyworker about it but not in great detail out of respect for her as a lady. The two ladies that I communicated with did not share much about themselves and backed away. I wasn't sure why this was but was told that it might be because I was still married. I think one of them was in a relationship and the other not long out of one, not a good one at that.

At that time my finances were in a state and they're not much better now. This I'd do worry about and Marta said she's surprised that I can sleep at night but, surprisingly, I somehow do. My spending now is quite a lot more under control although I have a long way to go. I'm paying off my debts slowly. A big mistake I made recently was that my bank gave me a £700 overdraft facility which caused me to practically go off the rails again. If I have it, I spend it. I learned something useful in one of the workshops that I attended a while ago and it was advice about worrying. We were told that most people worry and it is best to write your worries down and you will find, more often than not, things are not so bad and you can't do much about it anyway.

I continue to look for relationships here in Bedford but so far, no luck on the websites. I realise that I have to be patient and maybe the right lady will come along one day. My days back then were as busy as ever with voluntary work, meetings and workshops. At present, I attend four or five AA meetings each week, one on Tuesday lunch time, sometimes on Tuesday and Wednesday evenings plus, my home group at Ampthill on a Friday evening. Often, I'll go on a Sunday evening. I have learnt through the AA programme that there is no time for complacency or arrogance.

Some while ago, I had an unpleasant experience with a psychiatrist who I have never seen before. To this day, I don't know why I went to see him but I always like to keep appointments. Both Marta and our youngest daughter asked me why I went. This man I found very strange because he did not listen to what I was saying and kept contradicting himself on more than one occasion. In fact, I found him quite abrasive. He tried to suggest that I go on stronger medication. I was still waiting for my results from the professor. He'd told me they'd take about three weeks to come through. I queried the suggestion about stronger medication and he agreed not to increase them. After telling him that I had been through various tests including a memory test, he said they were a waste of time. He then put me through a memory test and, being confused, I didn't do very well. When I next saw my GP and told him about all this, he told me not to worry because I wouldn't be seeing that man again. So it has proved to be. Every other doctor has shown immense understanding and patience with me.

A little more about my relationship with Marta. As with all relationships, they change and evolve. Perhaps because we don't live together, it makes life easier. I still love her and guess that I always will and I believe that we are soul mates. Our relationship is more mature now and obviously not about sex. It's more about caring and being there for one another. She does not make it easy because she is rather secretive and is invariably late when visiting which is one of my obsessions. I don't comment on it now and just try to laugh it off. I have just remembered a part of her character that is truly Pisces. Her and our youngest daughter are both very caring towards me despite my difficulties. Their tolerance is amazing. I had an interesting experience when I was introduced by someone from the SPMH team. She was extremely thorough and instead of the interview being for forty five minutes, it went on for two hours and ten minutes. Towards the end she asked if I had thought about committing suicide. Fortunately I was able to say no but I knew someone who did think about it from the wellbeing centre. I was asked to report the matter which I did at the next opportunity. I have never seen the lady in question again but if I did, I wouldn't mention it to her unless she mentioned it first. As far as I am concerned, that is the end of the matter.

Throughout this tale, I have hardly mentioned my sister! As is my way, we've not been that close except for a couple of occasions. When we were young, I used to protect her from dodgy boyfriends sometimes, without success! It was lovely when she came out to Zambia and, of course, that's where she met her, now deceased, husband. He unfortunately developed bone cancer but, he was very determined and lived for about four years after his bone marrow transplant. I can relate one example of his determination and humility. I was in his study on a visit one day and there were a number of trophies on his shelf. I casually pointed to one and asked him how he had won it. He said he had won it two weeks earlier on a local golf course. He showed no pride but continued to practice in his garden that had a long stretch of grasd,concentrating more on his accuracy than the length of the drive. He obviously beat people younger than himself. The cancer had made an old man of him and he walked with a stoop. He was a loving family man with three children and several grandchildren. He passed away after a bout of pneumonia followed by a stroke which was just too much and he only survived for ten days afterwards. The medication had caused him to hallucinate but all his family were with him at the end. I decided not to ring my sister every day but checked in on her every few days so as to give her some space. When it came to his funeral I was in a quandary as to whether to go or not because a lot of people from far and wide would be attending. He had a lot of UNICEF work colleagues who would want to go. How would the family arrange transport from airports and where would all these people be staying? On Sunday the situation was resolved when his eldest child rang and said that I need not come because they would not have enough people to be with me. I took that as a kind gesture. I had not realised that in Scotland, funerals, or as I prefer to call them, celebrations, are arranged more quickly than in England. I had been preparing my mind to go there after two weeks or so had passed. I went into panic mode when it was decided to hold it within a few days. I found out through Facebook that it was to be held in six days. He had done a lot of good work in his life, starting off in Nepal then Somalia, Yemen, Iraq, in the no fly zone and finally back to Nepal again. I again found out through a Facebook post that between his first tour of Nepal and his return, infant mortality had reduced from 300 per 1000 to 30. This was a brilliant achievement and the government in Nepal needs to have a strong input too.

After two years I managed to visit and walked with my sister through the area where his ashes had been scattered. I made one failed attempt. I got myself to Luton Airport and due to my poor mental health I missed my flight although I had arrived there with ample time. It was due to my lack of focusing. Without checking the ticket I chose the flight that happened to be the one after mine. I was pretty devastated and my sister wasn't best pleased although she's come to terms with it now. I couldn't blame her for it because she had made a three hour round trip to pick me up. I would miss a flight again under different circumstances some time later. Also because of my mental health, anxiety and worrying intend to be rather unreliable but have improved somewhat in this area now.

Life continues to be interesting in Bedford and I continue to make more friends. I have been thinking about how fortunate I am over the last few days or so. I have perhaps a total of about eighty friends and obviously some acquaintances. But, as with most people, I value those special ones of which I have two or three in AA. One is a young lady to whom I was very attracted. She works in a local café /takeaway and is always pleasant and willing to chat. She is now married with a young son so I don't see her anymore. She is certainly pretty but not beautiful with an open face and a nice sense of humour. I would make a point of seeing her most days and sometimes buying something in the café. I have given her perfume and flowers on occasion too. A good while ago now, she invited me to their new home to give her some advice on the garden which was a bit of a mess but not too bad. If the grass was strimmed and raked it could then be regularly cut. There were also two or three trees which didn't need any work. I gave her the telephone number of someone who might be able to do the work. I haven't seen her since so I don't know if the work was ever done. What I found interesting was that although they had only been there a few weeks she had already made it homely.

Another lady was somewhat older and had an Italian partner and two children. She ran a small café near where the previous lady worked. The café became my favourite place to have a cup of tea. She is very friendly with a nice sense of humour and runs a proper family business. We chat and have quite a lot of banter and they tolerate my strange sense of humour. Her son found another job working at a local carvery so can only be there part time. The café is also a takeaway, she gets very stressed because she also prepares most of the food herself. I don't know how she manages but she always has a smile on her face. I bought her a cheap orchid just to show appreciation of our friendship. She told me something personal which rather surprised me at the time. I couldn't understand what she was saying to me until I knew the details. I met her partner who is a very busy man with seven businesses to run, including a pub and importing bricks from Holland. Unfortunately she fell out with someone at a neighbouring restaurant and, being a sensitive person, decided to put the business up for sale. She was thinking of retirement. Unfortunately I didn't see her anymore. However, I did bump into her a few weeks ago which was nice.

A while back, because of my precarious financial state, I began to go and collect food from a food bank which Marta did not approve of. She said there were more needy people than me and she may well be right. The situation is entirely of my own making. I went perhaps a couple of times and still have some of the food today. Every evening I go to a soup and sandwich kitchen except for Fridays when I go to my AA meetings. It takes place at what they call the old taxi rank. On Saturdays there are hot meals and refreshments plus takeaways including read, fruit and veg plus sandwiches etc. All donated by local supermarkets and cafés. In this way, some of my basic needs are met, free of charge.

At Florence Ball House where the OPMH team operate from, I used to go for an English breakfast for £1. After a while I stopped going because I felt that the meal was rather unhealthy. I now go for a healthier early lunch at a local day centre. At Florence Ball House they are refurbishing the kitchen so I do go there on a Saturday for a coffee and treat it much like a social. All of these things serve to make me aware of the generous things that they do for the needy in Bedford and I have only mentioned but a few so far.

When it was discovered that I had high blood pressure I was sent for an ECG test which involved attaching sensors to my chest which then fed into a monitor. I had to carry the monitor in one of my pockets. I had thought that the test would be done there and then but it was actually carried out over a twenty four hour period. It was a bit inconvenient, particularly when in bed, as the wires were rather intrusive going here, there and everywhere. I managed to carry out my day much as usual. One interesting thing was that a Zimbabwean lady attached the sensors for me and I told her about some of my experiences in Zambia and of my travels in Africa. She told me a bit about herself. She told me her name which in her local language means 'what I asked God for' I think that is a lovely turn of phrase. Her mother must have thought about it while she was pregnant and it was particularly relevant because the infant mortality rate is quite high in Zimbabwe.

Back at the rehab I would tell my key worker how many people I had spoken to that day. Some days it would only have been fifteen or so and I counted that as a big deal. Now I probably have about 240 friend's numbers in my mobile of which, maybe half are AA members.

My voluntary work in care homes gives me immense pleasure and I'm inspired by the caring staff. Some of the residents are happy to engage with me quite often, in the communal areas. Some, due to memory loss can be reticent. I have to remember that I'm not there to interrogate but to gently question as they become more used to me. Until eventually it becomes a natural conversation with the odd question along the way. Volunteers would be invited to barbecues, open days and fetes where a gentleman would sing and play his guitar on most occasions. Of course, he would choose songs that the old folk were familiar with and try to get them to sing along. I love being a part of the care family, as one manager calls it. Maybe three is my lucky number since I attended three barbecues and fetes a few years ago. These are the lovely benefits I receive from doing unpaid work.

My colleague and friend married a Zambian man who I believe I had got to know during my time there. He was mayor when I was working at the nearby settlement scheme. She was a nurse there and I visited in the North of the country. A Dutch man did the driving because it was quite a distance. It was very memorable and it was nice to see her, she made us quite welcome. In fact, I wrmt to their wedding with my mum in Royston back home. We stayed in a hotel overnight and I remember the noise of the trains shunting about not far away. Consequently, she now has quite a complicated surname, difficult to spell and pronounce. When I went on Facebook recently, I had some luck and put my phone number there. I was able to renew my friendship with her brother. We had lost contact for forty-eight years. He has not had an easy life with regards to the fruit farm and his quite large family. But he is quite resilient and his patience won through eventually. We would get together when he was in Bedford and also at their home after I had attended the AA committee in Baldock. It was nice to reminisce about our time in college and in Canada but don't do that too much because it is the present and future that we prefer to talk about.

More recently, I lost his landline and mobile numbers when I changed my phone. But, as before, I resorted to messenger this time to get in touch. This was via the lady in Holland Marsh near Toronto whose husband we had worked for all those years ago. Unfortunately, she lost her husband from a heart attack rather suddenly but she has a big family for company. She also knew the girl, now a lady, who I fell in love with on the picnic afternoon. It is wonderful that I have re-engaged with people from all those years ago. So hopefully that I'll see Ken and his wife on a regular basis. They also once came to Bedford where I was appearing in a theatre production about a year ago.

The theatre production developed out of the book store workshop and was a most amazing experience. Myself, and probably about five or six others were involved in meetings with two facilitators. We went through a process of ice breaking and we got up to allsorts such as one to one's, concentrating on eye contact. We would talk about one special experience and carried out activities such as flocking as a shepherd and his sheep or removing a coat with the help of a partner. We did other things that I can't remember because they packed so much in and there were six sessions held once each week.

One Saturday we went to Bedford school where we gave a talk about clothes. We then went to the swimming pool where we were encouraged to swim under water and be videoed. These videos were shown at the back of the stage during the theatre production. I had an interesting experience with my confidence and managed to float and relax for the first time in my life.

Then came the day of the theatre production having done some intensive rehearsals the previous week. The production was called 'Mind Me' as in respect for myself and others. We did many of the movements that we had done in the sessions and a few of us spoke about some personal experience. I spoke briefly about my problems with drink. After the production the audience were invited to ask questions. Some frie, including Ken and his wife were there which was nice. Prior to the final rehearsal, I had a meal with Ken and his wife along the river embankment.

One thing that surprised me was that I was more tired after the rehearsals than I was after the production. I guess this was down to confidence and just going with the flow.

I used to like my reading because it enabled me to learn new things. Since recovery, I have read both the bible and the Quran from cover to cover. I found nothing divisive in the Quran. When doing these readings I receive little messages. A while back I bought a book about the gardens of England because I was attracted by the front cover. It showed what I consider to be, the iconic bridge at Stanhead near Yeovil in Wiltshire. I visited there at least once on my own when visiting my sister when they lived in the area. I went there again with Marta when we were returning from a holiday by the sea in the West Country. We just thought that it would be a nice place to visit on the way home. So it proved to be and we went on a long walk around the lake and past the grotto. I have a lovely photo of Marta with her typical pose with her ipad on her arm. Behind her was the iconic bridge. This is why I was attracted to the book and it only cost £1 in a charity shop.

Stonehead is a National Trust property that reminds me of the amenities lecturer at college because he became a gardener for the National Trust. Another book I bought at the same shop had the signature of Sir John Guilgud on the inside cover which was a lovely surprise. There happened to be a lady standing there and she overheard the conversation I was having. She immediately googled on her phone and discovered that the book could be worth £29. So I took it to the local auctioneers at the next convenient occasion but they told me that it had no value and I was naturally disappointed.

Now, a while ago I bought a book called The Christian Agnostic and was attracted to it because the title is quite a contradictory term and also again, it was only £1. Anyway, inside the cover I saw a message from a couple to their doctor in Bedford. I guess their GP was a wonderful man. It was over forty years old and thanked the doctor for his care during the wife's recent illness. It was so nice to find this message in a Christian book. The book was from a Methodist perspective and I later gave it to our Methodist Minister who has helped me with my recent troubles along with our Methodist Superintendent. These are lovely experiences and memories.

I know it can be a cliché to say that there's always somebody worse off than yourself but you see it every day. It was particularly the case about a month ago when I asked a gentleman in a local rehab why he was pushing his wife in a wheelchair around the lawn. When I met him at an AA meeting he told me that his wife had severe arthritis which affects her back and puts her in a lot of pain. The best she can do is walk with a stick. She also went on to say that she drank too much but does not go to the fellowship. She refuses to go when he has suggested it. There are similarities with my wife.

More recently, I met a gentleman at a coffee morning drop in place. He had become blind a year ago due to a detached retina and I guess he will never see again. He was very calm and accepting of his situation. He told me something quite interesting about when he was recently on holiday in Turkey with a friend. He said they have a groove alongside the footpaths so he could just pop his stick in there and be guided on his way. Something for us to think about.

One thing I decided to do was to be kinder to myself and to take life a bit slower. I think I need to at my age although I don't find it easy. When I was at school I learned the word 'shad' which means to get dressed as quickly as possible. So this led to rushing about when in North America then Zambia and other countries. When I was in Milton Keynes I was well known for always asking when things would be done. I called my company Kirkman Flyers. Things are not all negative and I believe that I have achieved quite a lot. There have been areas where I have been patient with myself. I was patient in starting my own business but I did try to take short cuts on occasions. This sometimes got me into trouble because I would have to redo work which, with hindsight, I have come to regret.

The next occasion was partly forced upon me by circumstances and before I found a wife and got married, I was in my forties. My dad had to wait until he was fifty and when he finally married, it caused quite a stir within the family. Speaking of Marta, I have another amusing story to relate. One summer, a few years ago we went to the theatre in London and stayed overnight in a hotel. On the way back I saw her daydreaming as she looked out of the train window on a lovely summer day. She ran her tongue over her lips as a baby might do and I could see that she was having a little think. I said to her, 'I don't know what you are thinking but I know what I am!' After she nodded, I went on, 'you're very indecisive aren't you?' Tinehich she replied,

'yes.' I asked her how she'd ever managed to agree to marry me and she just looked at me and said absolutely nothing. This so amazed me, her look said that she wished she hadn't. I love her teasing ways!

Then there was the time when we were trying to find a new family home. I guess we were looking for about six months but we eventually found the right one. Marta still lives there today with a couple of cats and a rabbit. One Saturday afternoon we arrived at a four bedroom house at the edge of Milton Keynes. I turned to the family and said, 'I think we've found the right one.' And so it proved to be. It was owned by an old couple who had kept it looking like a show home although it was two or three years old. As well as having an en suite shower room it had a double garage, conservatory, a large private garden and ample parking. I was able to install double gates at the side of the house and put up a greenhouse and where I could store my truck and trailer, well out of sight.

Lastly, I showed patience with my recovery. I was so sick that I had to take small baby steps. As my alcoholism increased, I lost interest in myself, my family and my friends. I thought that drink was my best friend. I came to hate it but didn't know how to stop. I have come to realise that it may also have been because of my bipolar condition. I sabotaged everything including my marriage. Of course, I cannot justify this behaviour as I cannot justify the things that I get up to today. So, in a rather roundabout way, it is the seed of some of these thoughts of me trying to take things a little bit easier these days. But I don't find it easy. I find it difficult to do nothing but I can meditate in certain situations. I am bipolar of the manic type and often think it would be good to try and slow down. Scanning books is a symptom of this as well as my scratching spot.

Now I shall move on to a very special lady, not my wife as she will always be the best for me. I came to know this lady through the AA fellowship and she is of a similar age to me but has many years of sobriety. I will call her 'Tracy' in the interest of anonymity. It's the way of the AA and us best for the purposes of this. I have done the same for people who are alive today because I don't want them to be hurt by anything I have written. I seemed to see her more after I was suspended from the Bedford meetings. I was forced to attend meetings outside of the Bedford area. I began going to another group and started to see her more because it was her home group and I soon made it mine too. It happened because I noticed that the chaos who used to bring the milk had stopped attending regularly so I volunteered to buy it. This led on to other things like making it my home group. You hold various positions such as day refreshments, setting up the room, a welcomer, secretary, treasurer, representative and literature Secretary. I have done most of these at other meetings.

Tracy did a 'share me' evening and I was very impressed with her message, as were many other people. I would see her every week at the meetings and sometimes at other meetings. One Friday, there were some unexpected road works so I was running late and rang her to pick up some milk on my behalf. Along the way, she has given me a lot of help and encouragement. This has led me to take up three service positions. The first as secretary for one month on a regular rota basis. It was rather astounding at one group conscience meeting, that they asked me to stop chewing gum which is something I have done for years! But, I took their advice and I don't chew gum today. I told Marta and she said she had been asking me to stop chewing gum for years!

Along the way I was asked to take up two further positions, one was group service representative where I attend other groups to represent our meeting. I also have to report on the health of the group, take questions to intergroups etc. The latter has not happened so far. The intergroup meetings are held every three months. I also represent our intergroup at the regional meetings which I have attended four times now. I find it truly inspiring regarding the service that other members do. I think there were forty-two people at the last meeting giving up three or more hours of their Sunday. Some of them had come long distances in order to attend. I take advantage of being in Baldock and go to visit Ken and his wife after the meeting, they are very hospitable and make me very welcome. At one point, we had an intergroup meeting where we tried to define our positions. For a while, the meetings have been a bit of a mess with some people putting personalities before principles as we say. The AA principle is to work from the bottom up, hence the upside down triangle of unity service and recovery, without meetings, the AA would fall apart. I am glad I was not the intergroup chairperson during those difficult times. I would not be strong enough with discipline, bringing people to order and I prefer to stay in the background. I am happy with what I do and like to go with the flow, but, I will stand up for my principles if challenged.

As I have written, I quite like myself these days and feel much more at ease in the company of most people. I have become a bit of a social animal now I'm in recovery, I find life a lot different to when I was younger. I am a person of opposites, or a Jekyll and Hyde as we say in the fellowship. Sometimes, when I'm on my own I become quite anxious and do some scratching. Once I get out and about socially that anxiety melts away. I like nothing better than sharing some jokes as I have today. I will talk to anyone as long as they are respectful to me. This upset Marta sometimes as, by nature, she is shy. I usually have a smile on my face when I leave the flat and am generally a happy person these days. I have so much to be thankful for, not least my sobriety. I believe all of these things are God given.

I don't fully understand why things got better when I was out and about but some of it is to do with self confidence and thinking of others. Unfortunately, I still have a bit of an ego sometimes thinking I know it all, but that has reduced recently as I work through the AA programme which keeps me grounded. Sometimes, my anxiety is so bad that I dry retch as I walk away from my flat and I often get a dry mouth. My negative thoughts are generally unfounded when I review my day and so it is quite unwarranted. I have pretty good physical health for my age and usually get a good night's sleep, and the odd dream! I am eating more healthily in general and suffer from old age spread! I take vitamins and evening primrose in the evening helps me to sleep but that's not usually necessary now, I tire quite easily. I still walk quite a lot around town but sometimes, as I have today, I have an afternoon nap.

I was especially busy when doing the first Elves day for the alzheimer's society about eighteen months ago and it was good all round. When children confused me with Father Christmas it was funny! My family bought me an Elf outfit from Amazon which was generous of them. When I googled elves, I was informed that they were mystical little fellows and quite naughty like me! They usually live at the bottom of the garden. I found a Christmas cracker with a joke that asked, 'where does father recover after Christmas?' Answer? 'The elf hospital!' All good fun. I sent these various jokes to the alzheimers society after I had shared them over the phone.

A few years ago, I met a gentleman at an event at the local Quaker Centre. Various people used the rooms for different purposes and of course we had the AA meetings there. We had sadly had to leave the SA because numbers had dropped. This meeting, ironically, is much better attended and we are fully self sufficient. I was there in the role of treasurer for the meeting at that time. I got into conversation with the gentleman, Hussein, and his wife. He was English but had a Subad name and was a practising Muslim. His name was actually given to him by the Indonesian founder, Babak. He had what we would call a spiritual awakening and had set up the Sabul fellowship.

Babak was born in 1905 and I believe that he passed away in the late 1980's. He managed to carry the message throughout the world. It is not a religious organisation but a combination of Buddhism and the Muslim faith. It is about spirituality and opening the soul to God's faith. Being interested, I visited once a week for three months because he was what they call, my helper, he still is. This enabled me to understand the concepts. I was also given books to read in my spare time. I read a little every morning upon arising as well as my AA readings. When my mind is settled and open to information. When we meet, we have about fifteen minutes of quiet time then we do what is described as walking with the spirit. Men and women do this separately and you can do anything you like but try to avoid touching anyone. I tend to sing, think about life and talk to God and myself. I also think about Jesus and those who are important in my life, both living and deceased. You can do this for any reasons such as relationships, financial problems and work issues. I hope that in the long run, it will reduce my anxiety. After about three months I committed myself but it is still early days. At one meeting, I got a lovely warm feeling throughout my body. When I went to my first meeting where I was 'opened' as they call it, there were quite a few people there from outside of the area and we had refreshments afterwards.

At a later meeting, I had an interesting experience. I asked if I could have a Sabul name and if they would choose it for me but they said that I should choose it. I know a gentleman whose name is Iqbal and said that I would like to use that name. I was told that it means servant of God. How lovely is that?! Sometimes, they have wider gatherings and congresses and there can be people from all over the world and it can go on for three or four days!

Another recent experience that I found most interesting. When seeing my psychiatrist the last time, while waiting, I got talking to another patient. He knew some of the same people that I also knew. He spoke about a gentleman named Alan who is a committed Christian. He then told me that Alan is able to talk in tongues. On the way back from the meeting, I asked Hussein about this. He told me that we do that in the meetings and then I realised that I had innocently been doing it myself. Speaking in English mixed with Slovak and French. Some of it of course, is gibberish but all of it is in praise of the Almighty.

Another activity that I tried to get involved with four years ago was to do voluntary allotment work through The Present Day Centre. They help the homeless and lonely who often have mental health or substance abuse issues. For some reason it went nowhere but recently, I enquired again and now I do it once a week on Friday afternoon. Sometimes they also do work for the local community, clearing and replanting small public areas. Some of the other people were difficult to motivate and a little unreliable. I don't always agree with all of the horticultural practices but, as a newcomer, decided to make no comment unless they asked. I was not the boss but the plan was to stick with it but because of lack of interest and funding, I fear it is falling apart. All these sorts of things are done to try and raise people's self esteem.

Now, something that one may call a coincidence, but it did occur at a difficult time in my life. When I was suffering from extreme anxiety, I missed my plane to Scotland to see my sister. I then enrolled on an Alpha course. I got to know of it through an Anglican church that I used to visit once in a while because it is quite near to my flat. Two ladies from this church used to come to the prayer meeting at the Methodist church on a Monday morning. I believe that God guided me to this course at that difficult time. At this time also, I told a Croatian lady who works in a care home, of my anxiety. She rested her hands on my shoulders and we prayed together for my anxiety to be taken away. I think we met twelve times for the Alpha course and there were about five of us and two facilitators, a man and his wife.

Each time we met we would watch a video, this would be followed by a discussion about it and what it meant to us as individuals. On the final Saturday was spent at the home of one of the ladies and her husband. We were well looked after and given lunch there too. The topic on this last occasion was The Holy Ghost and how it could change your life. I will always remember the video that they showed us that day. It was about a man who was a thug and carried knives wherever he went. He was eventually arrested and put in prison. There, he stabbed a warden and was put into solitary confinement, he was considered a lost cause. He was made to attend an Alpha course. He thought that he had nothing to lose and was better than being in a prison cell. He didn't like God and went with a negative attitude. Over a period of time he was converted and is now a married man with two children. He does Bible study with them every evening. A life changer.

As we had our discussion, one person commented that the man had been visited by the Holy Ghost on at least two occasions during his difficult time. I believe that the same happened to me when I was going through recovery from alcoholism and seems to be happening again regarding my anxiety. I was certainly less anxious and thinking differently, in a more positive way. I believe that it started when the Croatian lady laid her hands on my shoulders and prayed for me.

After this Saturday, things improved for a good while. The confused feelings, mood changes, being fuzzy headed and instability seemed to be lifting. It is rather difficult for me to describe in detail, as it is with most spiritual experiences, I sort of felt better and it seemed to be growing daily. The improving weather also helps which most people appreciate. I think the most important reason for this change, and certainly if it is sustained, is the prayers from others and, of course, myself.

The SA came to know of my plight and sent me a card saying

that I was in their prayers. I didn't know that they even knew my address. It was the last two sessions of the course that changed things for me.

Some time ago, I started to do something that I was advised not to do by my younger daughter and two good friends. This was to stop taking the mood stabilisers. I did it by slowly reducing the dose over about ten days and things started to improve. My life is about contradictions as I have come to realise. It has also been the case with my mental health issues, hence the name, bipolar.

I have forgotten to mention that as well as attending workshops every Wednesday, afterwards I go to a 'pop in'. We meet at a café and generally chat socially. In many ways, it is a peer group and we like to support each other.

About seven or eight months ago, things started to become quite difficult and I have now come to realise why. For over a month I was going through a nasty patch of anxiety mixed with manic behaviour. There are three things that trigger the behaviour. One is too much caffeine, the next is smoking and lastly, trying to do too much. As my sponsor says, 'easy does it, but do it.' I used to set an agenda for myself and thought I was being clever by being so active in my recovery. This led me to have a nervous breakdown which lasted about six weeks. I would not go out of my flat for fear of panic attacks. Marta was very good and brought me food because I was unable to go out shopping, I even lost weight. I used to stay in bed all day and felt ashamed of myself. I pushed friends away for that reason. I prayed for relief like never before in my life. Obviously I still had a psychiatrist and a support worker, although he is quite negligent because I haven't seen him for about eight months now. I told my psychiatrist that I need a new support worker. I have heard nothing for about three weeks but I won't let it rest if something positive doesn't happen soon.

The situation I find myself in now is more positive and I don't set myself agendas but I allow God to guide me in nearly everything I do. I also have that little mantra that helps. I like to think outside of the box, as I have for most of my life. I try to be flexible and try things that I haven't done before but, like many of us, I also need routine in my life.

Something happened on the New Year before last. I would normally have gone to an AA meeting because it was a Sunday. Instead, I stayed at the sheltered housing to be with some of the residents here. I was amazed by the generosity of one resident who brought plenty of nibbles and drinks. He brought home made alcohol as well but that wasn't for me. I was also shocked because some of the residents were popping pills etc and they're somewhat older than me! They stayed up late until after 12.30am to watch the fireworks on television. It was certainly an evening to remember!

Two other opportunities revolved around food. As I now belong to the SPMH team, I usually go for a £1 English breakfast at Florence Ball House where the doctors practice from. It's convenient as it is only about five minutes walk from my flat. After a while, I found the breakfast to be a bit too unhealthy and now take an early lunch instead, for free! Back at Florence Ball House, I met one of the helpers in town who told me that they were refurbishing the kitchen so now would only be offering tea and coffee. I now use it as a social event. When they have finished the refurbishment in a couple of months, I plan to go back again and hope that the breakfast will be more healthy. It would be nice to have some cheeses, fresh meat and yoghurt etc.

On a different occasion, I was in my car one Saturday and I noticed a lot of people around what they call the old taxi rank near the centre of town. I decided to stop and investigate. They were there because there were free meals on offer and allsorts of other things to take away including clothes, bread, fruit and vegetables and filled rolls etc. There was tea and coffee on offer and most was donated by local supermarkets. There is no reason why anyone in Bedford should go hungry.

Despite some difficult times, as I have mentioned, life is far from boring. I generally get good advice from many quarters, too many to mention. Probably the most important quarter is my family, especially Marta, my doctor, the rehab, my AA friends, church members and the people I meet through my voluntary work. I know that I will get better in God's time and that is a good thing to remember.

I am still in touch with the people from the theatre production through Facebook and messenger. I am involved with people who want to tell their life stories and connected to these, I attended a poetry meeting. I was surprised that I could write poetry for the first time in my life because the lines had to rhyme. I composed one at a meeting that I'm quite proud of. Another opportunity I was offered was to do an interview with a local radio station about my bipolar condition. But, so far this has not happened. They suggested that someone from Mind should be alongside me to explain what they had to offer.

With regards to my medication, I now understand that I was given them to reduce my mood swings. They worked for around two months. I began to have mood swings again which was rather unpleasant and I was also getting side effects from the tablets. I decided to stop one of the medications and I told one or two friends so they could keep an eye on me. I'm the event, it was unnecessary because I did start to feel somewhat better.

Due to my mental health, I dropped one or two of my voluntary commitments. I now only visit two care homes as opposed to three as before. I have stopped working at the café because I now do the voluntary allotment. I heard recently that the café has had to close anyway due to financial issues. I have also stopped going to the Quaker meetings where we used to have half an hour of quiet time followed by sharing a healthy lunch. I still do my regular AA meetings because I know that this is the most important thing that I need to do to stay sober. I attend peer groups and workshops at the wellbeing centre and attend the recovery college. So my days are a little easier now although still quite busy.

When I got back from the aborted trip to Scotland, I was not feeling too well. I didn't rest on my laurels and made an appointment to see my psychiatrist. I was pretty desperate. I knew that my regular doctor was on leave until May and this was early April. Why would I have missed the plane as I did? I was certainly a rather confused and unwell man. Rather than feeling sorry for myself and doing nothing, I started, on Tuesday, to ring for an appointment. By Thursday afternoon I had heard nothing. Things seemed to be not moving forward and I was becoming increasingly frustrated and rang my local MP. I had done this before under similar circumstances because I knew that he was interested in mental health issues. They were able to influence the outcome and I received an appointment in a short time.

Something a little different to the above, but also loosely connected occurred at that time. Due to the trauma of my unprofessional doctor, it caused my bipolar to be more exaggerated and our youngest daughter tends to agree. On the other hand, it is only my theory but the rehab also seems to agree. This encourages me to never think of having another drink.

My character tends to be quite obsessive regarding my relationships with both men and women. Ego or bipolar? Possibly a bit of both. But, it is still not an excuse. With my bipolar, I tend to interrupt conversations, but I have become aware of this. I try to take a step back before engaging in any type of conversation and if I do interrupt, I always apologise. If I saw a couple talking, I would say, 'excuse me' before going any further or say, 'could I have a word?' It also could be caused by my condition because I see that in others. I need to settle down and look at my core values and consider my lifestyle at my age and the things that I'm trying to do. In some areas of my life, some things are unmanageable and a lot of these things are about my manic condition. I often find myself leaving my flat very early, rushing around and congratulating myself on being clever. But, it has affected my mental health and general wellbeing. In the end, something will have to give as I swap one obsession with another. This I have not yet come to terms with.

Recently, I was unexpectedly called in to see my doctor. This was done by a text message. He is a hard- working and diligent doctor who mentors other doctors. As a result, he is only on duty for four days each week. I guess I did need to see him and possibly he had heard about some of my recent difficulties. When I arrived, he was surprised to see me because he hadn't arranged the appointment. However, we just reviewed my present situation and particularly, my lifestyle. But, in the end, my medication is prescribed by my psychiatrist but she was away for another week. I'm sure she would have a lot to sort out when she got back but I was prepared to be patient.

Two things concerning my medication. I was considering asking for one of them to be reduced or changed. I was taking 250mg every evening to reduce side effects. Someone I know, who also suffers from anxiety, uses cannabis drops to calm herself down. On consulting with our youngest daughter, it was considered to be not a good idea because of my addictive nature. I took her advice.

I think several of us have had groundbreaking experiences in the Book Store Worksop. One special experience for me was when the topic was 'The rucksack'. This being the concept of carrying a burden of guilt regarding our mistakes in the past. This is also a term we use in AA when we do Step four. We analyse our mistakes with our sponsor and, of course, God (of his or her understanding) We analyse our past with regard to our character defects such as sloth, dishonesty, fear, ego and jealousy etc. It is a freeing experience which, as I have previously mentioned, has enabled me to have several spiritual experiences. This is promised in the Big Book of AA. When I did the theatre production, I spoke briefly of the rucksack and my problem with alcohol. We were also encouraged to write short stories and poetry, as I have previously mentioned. We learned about metaphors and meditation.

With regard to my medication, things settled down for a while but I guess, like most of us, I will never be a hundred percent well. I didn't have those dreadful wobbles for a long while when I would become confused and tired relatively easily compared to other people.

I guess being in the workshop encourages me to tell the story of 'The Scent and the Flower'. To avoid repeating myself, I shall be brief. The Scent is what I experienced when I kissed Marta when I met her again in Bath after twenty two years. But then, the story doesn't end there. When there were some difficulties with our relationship, we agreed to meet up in a carvery that she liked. I was walking there, I knew a lady who had some Peace roses in her front garden and she allowed me to pick some. On the way to meet Marta, I picked a single rose and gave it to her. She was brutally frank with me, perhaps for the first time in our relationship and I took it on the chin. I call it being assertive and we all have the right to be so. Relative peace exists in our relationship these days. But, I was astounded a week or so afterwards when she visited, I saw the flower on the floor in her car. Wilted. It tells me that a relationship has to be nurtured and cared for in order for it to survive and grow.

Recently, I bought myself a new mobile phone and some numbers disappeared. One of these was Ken from my college days and I lost touch with him temporarily. He isn't on Facebook so I messaged his sister but she doesn't often check her messages. In the end, I messaged the lady in Canada whose husband we had worked for and she was able to put us in touch again.

I have been accepted as a Health and Wellbeing volunteer. A rather grand title for a welcomer and a facilitator. It is with an organisation called ACCM who basically help people from ethnic minorities with relationship problems and female mutilation etc. They also offer free ESOL courses and one hour of free legal advice. I visit them every morning of the week for a coffee although I have not been used as a volunteer there yet. There are games to play including card games, pick-a-stick and dominoes. There is usually a lovely relaxed atmosphere.

I have other voluntary jobs that I do occasionally for charities in Bedford. The first is with the Seventh Day Adventists who worship on a Saturday and prefer to be vegetarian and also to abstain from alcohol and caffeine. I first went there as what they may call a service user because it is a charity for the homeless, those in financial distress and the lonely. I fit into two of those categories. As I often do, from a service user, I become a volunteer and so it has been with the SDA. I began working as a volunteer after two meetings. It's called The Wellbeing Project and they try to put on a meal every other Tuesday if there are enough volunteers available. We are identified by our yellow t-shirts. They usually cater for around twenty people. After we have cleared up, we have a meeting to discuss the event and say a few prayers. As with many of these projects, I am inspired by what other people do without seeking praise. They have been very supportive of me regarding my anxiety and when I became ill again.

It is the same with the All Nations Church in Bedford which serves a meal for a similar reason to the SDA. They try to do this every other Sunday. They also have special events at Christmas, Easter and on some Bank Holidays. I only went for one meal there before I volunteered. Generally, not so many people attend so my services are not yet needed. I have made quite a few friends there, one man in particular called Pedro. He has been to my flat twice to visit me. He has an inspiring story. He went to rehab for alcohol and cocaine abuse. He relapsed when he came to Bedford. He told me that one evening he was visited by God while he was drinking whisky and taking cocaine. His desire for these addictions was taken away. He is now a strong and active member of All Nations and has a wife and two children. As with many charities, they do missionary work in less developed countries. They support an orphanage in Tanzania where he goes to show them how to do decorating work because that is his trade. He posted a picture on Facebook of himself and a young boy doing some decorating. The charity also does some work in Malawi.

The most recent workshop I attend is called Spirituality and Recovery Peer Group Support and is again held at the wellbeing centre. In January, I missed a session because I wasn't well. There are two facilitators and one comes from London although he has moved to Luton now. He has just become a new father and was away last week. Prior to the meetings we have about fifteen minutes of guided meditation. Afterwards we share about our previous month and good or not so good experiences in our lives. I find it useful and look forward to the sessions.

As I mentioned, I missed a session in January due to being ill. The warning signs began in December but I didn't realise at the time. It progressed until late January or early February. I had started to have panic attacks around Christmas time and eventually I had a nervous breakdown. For six weeks I was again unable to leave my flat and Marta brought me food and shopping. I felt totally emotionally drained and I couldn't even cry, much as I needed and wanted to. My psychiatrist put me on Sertraline and warned me that it could get worse before it got better. So it proved to be. I used to fall in the street as if I was drunk. On one occasion when I had had a really bad fall, I was helped the hundred yards or so back to my flat. Someone called for an ambulance but that wasn't necessary because I was back in a safe place. When I eventually plucked up the courage to go outside, our youngest daughter, who is very kind to me, said that I should be proud of myself. I used to call for help or an ambulance but that was a waste of time because they would never take someone to hospital for a panic attack. When I was informed of the costs involved, I stopped calling. Talking to people about my experience may have made it worse, having to be admitted to the hospital.

At the beginning I took baby steps because I was so unwell. I still am to some extent, some six months after. I'm not sure if it is a result of my situation or the side effects of medication. Throughout, I prayed to God more seriously than I have ever done in my life. So now I think of it as God who got me through this and the reason why I am here to tell this tale. The lady who laid her hands on my shoulders and prayed for me also prayed for me throughout this recent series of events. As did many friends as I was later told. Some may even have prayed without me knowing.

Another little update on Marta. She developed a nasty abscess on the bone in her jaw. She suffered so much that she had swollen cheeks and a double chin. She was on antibiotics for two weeks. More recently, she has had more problems with a trapped nerve in her neck. She has been operated on once which was very intricate and it may have to be done again. If it was to go wrong, she may be paralysed from the neck down. She is often in a lot of pain but is so brave and hardly complains. Her last operation fell on a Sunday and I was able to be there. I bought her a lovely pink Camellia with lots of buds on. I have never seen a more healthy one.

I can come to terms with my mental health and I know that the AA meetings help too. Now that I'm feeling somewhat better, I know I have to be careful because I don't want to go back there again. I feel that I can now empathise with people who have the same issues that I have. Maybe I can help them too. These days I let God guide me in everything that I do. Including whether to buy something or not. Being a shopaholic, it doesn't always work. I also try to take one day at a time and not project too much. My mantra also helps.

God stories. Things relating to God that I've experienced in my life. Obviously, my recovery from alcoholism is a miracle, as it is for so many people. Meeting Marta, of course, after all of those years, I consider to be a miracle. It is something I had prayed for. Then there was the time when we, as a family, used to visit Cambridge some Saturdays. After some lunch or a picnic we would visit a few churches. On one occasion, we entered the church to find a display board with photos of a project in Zambia. On enquiring we were informed that the project was going to preach in two weeks. I consulted the family as to whether we should come to the service and they agreed that we would. We heard him preach and then surprised him and his wife afterwards, telling them that we had heard his sermon.

On another occasion, our youngest daughter was coming to the end of her junior doctor training in Lincoln. She asked her mum and I if we would attend evensong at the Cathedral, of course we agreed. It was a traditional Anglican service but not many people were there. We sat in the choir stalls. After a few hymns and various readings the curate got up into the pulpit and gave a short address. He spoke of how God had helped when he grieved for the death of his father. He then spoke briefly about Job in the Old Testament and finally, he spoke about Jesus. He said, 'Well, these are the J people'. Next to me were sitting my wife and youngest daughter, both of whom have names beginning with the letter J. I consider this not to be a coincidence but chose to say nothing to them. Perhaps they are the two most important people in my life. Especially during my difficulties over the last nine years or so.

Now, some more recent relationships, some of which are still

22 IS MY LUCKY NUMBER

developing. Living on my own, I get rather lonely especially in the evening and overnight. I have sought ladies outside of my marriage. I have been on two or three dating sites without success. More recently, I have come to know two ladies under entirely different circumstances. One lady, I met in a café in Bedford. She is from South Africa and is in the care sector. She is very busy visiting sometimes fifteen hours a day. We are good friends but not so close.

The other lady I met on Facebook. She was a lady who posted lots of interesting stuff and our relationship developed from there. She is from Bangkok in Thailand where I have visited twice before when I was much younger. Although she was not able to meet me at the airport since it was the middle of the night, she recommended a basic hotel. It was close to where she lives. When I got up in the morning I had a haircut and a pedicure. Later in the afternoon, she came to visit me and we spent the evening chatting, some of the time in the hotel. We seemed to hit it off really well and she appeared to be very relaxed around me. She told me that she had been married with a daughter and her husband was an alcoholic who used to beat her up. She divorced him and he later died in hospital from his addiction. She vowed never to have anything to do with Thai men again. I can't remember what we did the next day but during the two weeks she kept me busy going here and there. The second evening she again came to my hotel. We had an intimate time together that we both seemed to enjoy and then she went back to her flat. She was very free with me and had no problems holding my hand in a public place. Perhaps the most memorable experience was when we went, on two occasions, to a temple to celebrate Buddha day. Worshippers bring plenty of food including rice. After some readings and talks, the monks, about six of them, would firstly enjoy the food and refreshments. Everything is cleared up, the floors swept. I found the Thai people to be very diligent in everything they did.

On the first day, she argued for a luxury minibus to take us to the beach. The beach was not so good but the swimming was adequate. We went with a close friend of hers who I had first met. She is also very happy, jokey and cheerful. She is widowed but under different circumstances. It was a lovely day out.

On another occasion we went to the King Old Palace but, unfortunately, for part of the time, it rained rather heavily and restricted our viewing. It was still a lovely experience and I have the photos to prove it. Her friend is an amazing lady and they both love taking photos. My lady friend is now planning to become a monk. To be honest, I've no idea what it involves or how long it will take to do it. I remain very close to her and we are able to communicate through messenger and WhatsApp. Although that is not always possible due to her phone having a virus. We plan to marry and she plans to build a house with her savings and we plan to create a garden together. I have never loved someone more and I believe that she is a gift from God. She has been sent to me so I should look after her the best way I can.

I was warned by my sister that some Thai ladies hold older, European men to ransom, taking all their money. She knows someone who was made homeless because of this. Since my sister has not communicated with me for some reason, I don't find it helpful. She has not enquired about the situation. She has come to this conclusion without asking questions. On the other hand, I have questioned my lady friend about her finances and her situation regarding building a house etc. I have told her that I have no money to invest in the house and she has accepted that. She says she will sell her flat and any extra money needed, she will borrow from a friend which I accept.

I will keep an eye on her as to any financial demands she may make from me. I have to protect myself at my age. I plan not to rush and I'll continue to visit every three months and see how we go. If things go well, I can see myself moving there in a couple of years or so. It will be a big thing for both of us, especially for me, making a new life in a foreign country. I don't know the Thai language but I'm willing to learn. I'm not sure if she mentioned if she also has bipolar. If she didn't, she certainly behaves as though she does, as I know from my own experience. She is so active in many aspects of her life and I will only mention what I know so far. There is her family life, various activities with her Buddhist faith, voluntary work with an old person's club, organic gardening, the gym and swimming. She also travels quite a lot, having recently been to South Korea and plans to go to Japan later in the year.

It is all so amazing to me and, thanks to social media, we usually speak twice a day and share other things. Although we are all these miles apart, I don't feel lonely. I guess that's what love is about… She is like a lovely dream for me so I hope I'm not being deluded. As I said, my sister is suspicious of this relationship and fair enough, so I have to continue to watch her. She is going to finance building the house, there is no way I can help with that and I must stay strong in that. She sent me a naughty message the other day. She said she would like to play golf with me, oil my shaft and play with my balls! Again, I'm a little suspicious as the quickest way to my heart is to offer me sex.

I will end this take on a positive note. Since I was in rehab I have gone to meetings and continued to do so in Bedford. Of late, more regularly. For two or so months, another member was having severe problems with his back. He was spending extended periods in hospital where I think he is at the moment. His only income is benefits and, considering that he's married with two children, it has put him under severe strain. Unbeknown to me, the other members collected about £1200 to help him out and if that isn't a sign of recovery I don't know

MR HEDLEY KIRKMAN

what is.

As a way of a little resume I would like to say how much I have enjoyed this writing. Considering at school I had little interest in English or reading. It surprises me that I am able to express myself with some ease. For me, it is not so much about my life but of how my experiences may help and encourage others who are going through, or have been through, similar experiences. As well as being fulfilling, writing this has been therapeutic and cathartic. I know that I often talk too much these days so I hope I haven't too much or repeated myself. I also hope that I haven't bored or confused you.

Now, I must go and find something to do to fill up my time. I do like to keep active…

END

ABOUT THE AUTHOR

Hedley Kirkham was born in Essex.

The year he entered the world was 1948.

This was the same year that the NHS was created along with The World Health Organization.

Both caring institutions and they very much reflect the writer.

Clive now lives in Bedford where he reads and, perhaps but surprisingly, does all he can for local charities.

MR HEDLEY KIRKMAN